McNutt's Island Journal

Elizabeth Walden Hyde

Edited and Introduced by Joanna Gilman Hyde

Pottersfield Press, Lawrencetown Beach, Nova Scotia, Canada

Library and Archives Canada Cataloguing in Publication

Title: McNutt's Island journal / Elizabeth Walden Hyde ; edited and with an introduction by Joanna Gilman Hyde.
Names: Hyde, Elizabeth Walden, 1933-1993, author. | Hyde, Joanna Gilman, editor.
Identifiers: Canadiana (print) 20220186693 | Canadiana (ebook) 20220186804 | ISBN 9781989725832 (softcover) | ISBN 9781989725849 (EPUB)
Subjects: LCSH: Hyde, Elizabeth Walden, 1933-1993—Diaries. | LCSH: Sheep ranchers—Nova Scotia—McNutts Island (Island)—Diaries. | LCSH: McNutts Island (N.S. : Island)—Biography. | LCGFT: Diaries.
Classification: LCC FC2345.M328 H93 2022 | DDC 971.6/25—dc23

Front cover images: Rock – Photo by Mille Sanders on Unsplash; Sheep – Photo by Astakhova on Vecteezy.
Back cover image: Photo by Martin Schmidli on Unsplash.
Title page image: Elizabeth Walden Hyde in front of the Evening Star stove in her McNutt's Island home in the summer of 1971.

Cover design: Gail LeBlanc

Pottersfield Press gratefully acknowledges the financial support of the Government of Canada for our publishing activities through the Canada Book Fund. We also acknowledge the support of the Canada Council for the Arts and the Province of Nova Scotia which has assisted us to develop and promote our creative industries for the benefit of all Nova Scotians.

Pottersfield Press
248 Leslie Road
East Lawrencetown, Nova Scotia, Canada, B2Z 1T4
Website: www.pottersfieldpress.com
To order, phone 1-800-NIMBUS9 (1-800-646-2879) www.nimbus.ns.ca

Printed in Canada

Conseil des arts du Canada | Canada Council for the Arts
Funded by the Government of Canada | Financé par le gouvernement du Canada | Canada
Arts Nova Scotia Nouvelle-Écosse
Nova Scotia

Introduction

My mother, Elizabeth Joan Walden Hyde, was born November 26, 1933, in Palisades, New York, and grew up in adjacent Snedens Landing where she had what she always referred to as an "idyllic childhood." She graduated from Nyack Public High School in 1951 and from Wells College, majoring in French Literature and Drama, in 1955. That year she and her parents, Howard Talbot Walden 2nd and Josephine Elizabeth Meadow Walden, and my mother's only sibling, Ernest Beverly Walden, took a family drive to Nova Scotia, in Atlantic Canada. They fell in love with the southwest shore of the province and bought a summer house in Jordan Bay, a small community near the nineteen-kilometre-long Shelburne Harbour.

The mouth of Shelburne Harbour holds the 1,800-acre McNutt's Island, shaped like a candle flame, and illuminated on its south end by the Cape Roseway Lighthouse. My mother and her brother occasionally sailed around McNutt's, where my mother's interest in the island grew enough to buy a piece of tax-sale property, sight unseen, with a wedding present from her marriage to childhood playmate Francois Michael Louis Tonetti Hyde in 1960. The land overlooked the western side of Shelburne Harbour and, to my mother's delight and surprise, included an abandoned farmhouse which has since become the only original structure left standing from when the island was once populated by about forty families over one hundred years ago.

After my birth in 1961 and a year in Africa ending with the birth of my brother Howard Talbot Walden Hyde in 1962 (who died unexpectedly on November 22, 2007, aged forty-five), our parents separated and later divorced. My mother moved us to Valley Cottage, New York, where annual summer trips to Nova Scotia began. When Howard and I were very little we stayed in Jordan Bay with our grandparents while our mother restored her island house (which would have no electricity and no plumbing) with the help of her father and one or two carpenters.

Back in Valley Cottage each fall and winter of the '60s, her continued interest in acting and a career in writing culminated in 1970 when an eighteen-month love affair with jazz musician Robert Sage Wilber (1928-2019) broke my mother's heart. She took refuge in the Jordan Bay house for the winter of 1971 to 1972, while renting the Valley Cottage house year-round, and enrolled Howard and me in the Sandy Point Consolidated School. She spent that year reworking the novel titled *Not Even The Moon,* written about her marriage during her time in Africa.

In 1973 she wrote articles for magazines and business journals, tutored, and then hired herself out as a substitute English teacher during a school strike in the Nyack Public School system in 1974. She discovered an appalling lack of instruction in English grammar and sentence structure and was compelled to acquire the credentials to become a full-time English teacher. In 1979 she received her master's degree in American Literature from Lehman College, and was certified to teach English and French in public and private high schools.

In 1976 my grandparents sold their house in Snedens and moved permanently to Jordan Bay, becoming landed immigrants of Canada until their deaths in 1979 (Josephine) and 1981 (Howard). My mother, brother, and I gained landed immigrant status in 1977, but it wasn't until the mid 1980s that my mother took advantage of her official permission to stay more than just summers in Nova Scotia.

While my mother treasured every summer on McNutt's, she often fantasized about the winters there and chose what would be one of the most difficult winters to take off from teaching, again renting the Valley Cottage house year-round, to embark on her hazardous, solitary adventure (which included her early involvement with island sheep). She and the Croft family, who kept the Cape Roseway Lighthouse, along with John the assistant, were the only year-round residents on the island. It was the winter of 1984 to 1985, for which she kept this journal. She stayed on McNutt's too for the winter of 1985 to 1986, when she sold the Valley Cottage house and bought a heritage house in Shelburne, the Shakespeare House, which I and my first husband, Peter Lynn Haeghaert, restored for her. The winter of 1986 to 1987 was spent in the Jordan Bay house with my brother Howard and a few stray sheep who might not have survived the winter out on McNutt's.

My mother spent the late '80s on the island with her growing flock of sheep, a large vegetable garden, and frantic trips ashore to perennial flower beds at the Shakespeare House and to problems with rental-property tenants. Her first and only grandchild to be born in my mother's lifetime was Peter Lowe Haeghaert, born December 27, 1987, and I have only one memory of my mother having any time alone with him: taking him in his stroller to the bank.

In the spring of 1991, after being mysteriously unable to do her taxes, my mother had a brain hemorrhage after lugging a fifty-pound bag of grass seed out to McNutt's, alone, and when the blood re-absorbed over the summer, she was diagnosed with a malignant brain tumour on October 2, 1991. Her surgeon told me he didn't expect her to live beyond the spring. She lived a year longer, half-paralyzed, wanting to be taken out to the island on a stretcher, while her daughter, artificially "prepared" for her mother's inevitable death, could not bring herself to arrange such an outing.

My mother died in Roseway Hospital, Sandy Point, on March 27, 1993, at the age of fifty-nine. Her ashes were spread by my brother, in the form of her initials, in the Lower Orchard of her island house during what she called "Apple Blossom Time," beside a granite monument with an attached limestone squirrel from her mother's garden.

Joanna Gilman Hyde
March 2022

People Mentioned in the Journal

Editor's Note: Efforts have been made to identify everyone mentioned in the journal, but this was not always possible. Editor's explanations are in square brackets.

Bob Crofts: Robert Croft was the head lightkeeper at the Cape Roseway Light from 1983 to 1986. Elizabeth consistently refers to him as Crofts, with an s.

Barry and Lyndon Crowell: Barry was the assistant Cape Roseway lightkeeper from 1962 to 1977 and Lyndon was his son.

Nathan Demings: a carpenter from Carleton Village and son of Mrs. Demings, the former owner of the house. She had told Elizabeth she might as well put a match to it when Elizabeth discovered the house on her tax-auction property and asked the Demings if they were certain they didn't want the house.

Hal Dozier: the son of friends from New York. In the early 1970s Elizabeth had a "settler's agreement" with some of her friends and her brother whereby purchasers of her 50-acre lots were obligated to not subdivide but to build a small dwelling to declare ownership. Hal built an unfinished log cabin on one of the lower grants on the west side of the island.

Amos Hagar: built Elizabeth's boat landing in the 1960s and owned property on McNutt's Island.

Louis Hemeon: owned a house at the north end of McNutt's, which Ruth VanBuskirk (Mrs. Van) fixed up in 1967 or '68.

Francy: Elizabeth's husband, Francois Michael Louis Tonetti Hyde (1932-2012). They separated and later divorced.

Joan King: a family friend of Elizabeth's parents. She lived in Shelburne and her son Barry was Elizabeth's chartered accountant. Her son Colin is also mentioned, as well as his then girlfriend, Sheila Deinstadt.

Evelyn La Ban: Elizabeth's cousin on her mother's side, who lived in Englewood, New Jersey.

Little Man: the little high-pitched voice from Elizabeth's small weather-band radio she would place on her chest to listen to the marine forecast every night in bed. She would often go to sleep that way.

Nick Lyons: a New York publisher, president of Nick Lyons Books from 1979 to 1984 and Lyons & Burford Publications from 1984 to 1998.

Mary Ann Miles: nicknamed Mousie and one of Elizabeth's settlers.

George and Susie Miller: caretakers of Elizabeth's parents in Jordan Bay.

The Perrys: Walter, Ron, and Ron's son Marc.

Tom Peterson: from Jordan Falls, built the *Molly* in 1966 or 1967. He also built and sold to Elizabeth a much smaller boat in 1985 that she called "Tom's boat."

Anne Barclay Priest: author of *Trafficking in Sheep* and a friend of Elizabeth's, who raised sheep on Blue Island, eight kilometres from McNutt's. She helped Elizabeth move the Prizer Regal stove from New York to McNutt's.

Brian Race: carpentry instructor. His wife was Rilla.

The Sandy Point Guys: fishermen at the Sandy Point wharf, about ten minutes from Shelburne.

The Scott family: Phil Scott was a champion log roller and owner of Scott's lumber mill in Barrington.

Waldo Stoddart: one of the "Cape Islanders" from Cape Sable Island. He had a camp down the road from Elizabeth's house.

Tony: Harry Runette, a friend of Elizabeth's who lived on a tiny island in Westport, Connecticut. He was in love with her and she "married" him in a New Year's Eve ceremony in 1991 at the Shakespeare House in Shelburne where she was living after her brain tumour diagnosis.

The Vans: the VanBuskirk family. Van (Harry, the head lighthouse keeper at the Cape Roseway Light from 1966 to 1983) and Ruth are the parents of Skipper, Tanya, Cliff, Dwight, and Gail, five of their eleven children. Graham is Ruth's brother and Skipper's namesake.

Dan Walden and Aunt Ellen: Dan was Elizabeth's uncle on her father's side. It was Dan's wedding present of $100 which Elizabeth and her husband Francois Tonetti Hyde used to buy the original 250 acres, including the McNutt's Island house, at a tax auction in 1961. Ellen Walden Demarest was Dan's sister.

Bob, or Wilber: Robert Sage Wilber was a musician Elizabeth loved even years after their eighteen-month relationship ended in 1970.

Elizabeth's Boats

Molly was built and launched in 1966 or 1967. She was named for Mollie (Mary) Sneden (1709-1810), who, from 1758 until just before her death, ferried people across the Hudson River at a point twelve miles up from New York City, thus originating the name of the hamlet Snedens Landing where Elizabeth and Francy grew up.

Elizabeth's father, Howard Walden Talbot 2nd, built three square-ended punts named *Wynken, Blynken,* and *Nod,* after the children's rhyme.

Elizabeth's Pets

Mac and his litter mates Minnie, Murtle, and Moe were the products of Mary, a shaggy medium-sized dog Elizabeth got for Joanna and Howard for Christmas in the late 1960s, and

Sammy, a short-haired, short-tailed terrier who lived across the street in Valley Cottage. Mac became Elizabeth's "white-haired boy" with a "hiney handle" – a medium-sized tail (though Sammy had what looked like a docked tail).

Timmy was a wharf kitten, white with orange patches, who followed Elizabeth and her family into the *Molly* one day. She gave him to her father, who initially didn't want him but then started feeding him a soft-boiled egg each morning. Annabelle was a stocky little orange cat who came from neighbours in Valley Cottage who had more than twenty cats.

Elizabeth's Stoves

The Prizer Regal, the main cooking stove that Elizabeth brought from New York, replaced the Master Climax, which was the name on the white oven door of the original wood stove in the kitchen. Elizabeth liked the name so much that when she replaced the stove with the Prizer Regal, she retired the Master Climax to the shed, where it remained until after her death.

The Franklin, her wood stove in the living room, replaced the Evening Star, which was moved upstairs. She did intend to hook it up to the upstairs flue and during a cold snap in February of 1985, she mentions having "all three working for a while," so at some point the Evening Star must have been operational in the upstairs of the house. She was able to heat pots and make tea on the top of the Franklin.

McNutt's Island Journal 1
September 1, 1984 – November 12, 1984

September 1, 1984

Saturday before Labour Day, and on any other year we would have closed the island yesterday, returned maybe once today with laundered sheets or to call a missing cat, and had the boat hauled up at Sandy Point. Beer with the guys in farewell, punt and boat gear moved to Jordan Bay, car washed and frantic packing for departure.

But for me now, summer seems to be beginning. A warm calm day, freshened but not yet cooled, by an increasing northwest breeze. Am looking forward to saying *hello* to my Sandy Point guys on Tuesday when I'll sail around for the *first* time and hope for some mackerel. Homesick for the old crossing each time I glance across from the Carleton Village 330-155 crossing route (NNW x ¼ NW).

Instead of readying to go, I made the day memorable by bringing on a big Franklin stove ($50 from ad in *Coast Guard,* including pipe, elbow, reducing pipe and screen!

Cast iron and considerable weight.) Had nothing arranged, but the pick up into truck was manoeuvred with help of Henry next door to seller ([Henry] worked for Irving, was fired for boozing; now overweight. – used to butter me up and told Bob [Wilber] what a lucky man he was) – left all the car clutter, camping and fishing gear under Skipper's stairs. Asked Skipper, out on the water, if he "could" help me get it down with the truck. Skip then and there dived for his first scallop. A big one.

Delivered stove to Gunning Cove wharf, again assisted handsomely by Skipper arriving on motorcycle (after quest for him, to Van's, Fort Point), Stanley Demings and others, after fishermen I didn't know had helped me take it out of the car and onto wharf. Dwight and Skipper, Sheila – Colin's friend – her brother and little kids came in the speedboat to wharf and helped me hoist it into truck. And thus to house where it sits in front of the Evening Star waiting to burn our piles of logs that would never have gone in the kitchen stove.

Afterwards, went aboard the *Sally N* and admired all the woodworking – drawers, cupboards, laminated deck done by ...? Name? Les Nickerson? Anyway, his wife's name is Winnie, and the Captain sat smiling modestly over his handiwork: "Everything you see I built," looking ahead while he talked to me, and ordering his wife, who sat knitting a raspberry coloured sweater, to get us some coffee.

Later I tracked the entire north end for vanished rams – Mac straining at his leash – tearing my shirt and leg skin on branches. Found grazed areas that had never been before, and only the one dead yearling I had seen at the old house.

Home to admire the Franklin again and chuckle over Dwight's comments as it was heaved to the front stoop. "Whew, she's beginning to smolder."

September 2, 1984

Time to make lists. Summer projects not yet accomplished:

– *Molly* painted, sides and gunnel
– *Blynken* caulked and painted
– New oars served; one pair painted (Margin Note: leave till next spring??)
– Yard chairs repaired (including new brown one)
– lawn mower repaired. Finish grass cutting
– move burning bin
– kitchen chimney scraped, spackled, painted inside (Margin Note: remortared and plastered 1985)
– front living room windows and outside trim painted
– windows washed (shed especially)
– inside window sashes painted. living room; study
– Shed set up with board walls, pegs for tools
– workbench (Margin Note: organized 1985)
– move all tools (but bow saws, axes) out there
– move all putty, etc. from pantry shelves to kitchen commode
– Make room in connection way for coats, boots
– Make CLOSET space upstairs. Or elsewhere
– Refinish blanket chest (Note: JGH 1985) (put at top of stairs)
– commode in kitchen
– J's bow-front commode?
– Clean, oil, and repair sewing machine. Put in bedroom
– Mending clothes, cushions, etc.
– Sew new cushion covers. Blue/grey
– Glue: coffee table
– *READ* all old magazines!

– sheep drops, daily! Cover garden. Turn under (Note: Done '84 – repeat '85!)
– (outside:) eelgrass from landing: cover tarp. – weigh down horse manure, spruce boughs
– (Margin Note: got sidetracked) Path cleared of dead bay: all dead wood
– Clean out spring off path to boat landing
– " " " " " " lower orchard NEW WATER SOURCE!
– Dig, fertilize, plant and mulch flower bulb beds, south side house
– Dead old bay cleared from far meadow
– All small spruce trees cleared from far field,
– " " " " " along path
– " " " " " in front view /other fields
– Limb two fallen (2 yr.) trees – lower orchard
– " storm fallen trees (some remain 1985)
– Saw poles for firewood
– *WOOD*
– Move up old wood piles. Logs to front stoop.
– (every day!!!) Stove wood split from trunk logs Franklin woodpile built
– (spring) Saw new fallen boughs. Make brush pile.
– (spring) Split stove logs cut by F & H [Francy and Howard] (1985)
– *Fencing* – garden; currant bushes; gooseberries flower beds; fruit trees
– *Trail to Northeast Bluff* completed!
– *TREES DOWN.* All I can manage, lower orchard with bow saw. The rest with Scott family's help ??
– New *LANDING* Jonathan's Point.
– *INSULATION* over kitchen, around chimney and under eaves

– upstairs room. Length of ceiling sidewalls to peak
– cover hole, outside wall to North
– cover floor of storage space, with something to insulate
living room ceiling at edges
– Connection way: patch hole behind shingle barrel.
– Piece top of South door – or new door
– inset lower hinge – (chisel)
– *Storm Windows* Kitchen & bedroom (hinged; hooked)
(Living Room?)
– Paint them.
– Paint storm doors. Repair. Vapour barrier over screens for
upstairs.
– *COAL* – from light(house). (Move? 1985?)
– *Pickling Herring* – jars. Keep some salted for winter
– Stash away vegetables. Potatoes
– *APPLES* – to bins. Ask old fellers [McNutt's early settlers]
how.
– Carrots in wood shavings, sand
– Study *CHAINSAW* books. Use on trunks & poles.
– WOOD FROM ROAD
– TRANSPORT AND INSTALL NEW FRANKLIN
STOVE
– Hook "Evening Star" to upstairs flue (re-open hole)
– Drag new brick flue pieces from old house. Drag old brick.
– Build NEW FLUE for guest room. Find 2-plate top stove.
(Margin Note: What else?)
– EELGRASS AND SPRUCE BOWS around connection
shed, cellar door, pantry, guest room – kitchen, front
porch, living room, study, bedroom
– EVENING STAR: new flue hole upstairs?
– new flue (from fallen house) in guest room?
– LAMB SHED

Meanwhile, there is everyday fridge frigging, lamps to clean and fill, sheep walks to take and sheep to watch around the house, routine firewood and refuse chores (ashes, compost, dump, etc.) – and well tending (Two weeks now on the barn well.) along with trips ashore: lawyers, Lands and Forests; Highway Dept.

Any chance to do some writing/editing?

teaching ... ?

Nope, not even letters.

And now, back to the fridge. New wick has been wrecked by carbon build-up during 4-day sheep gather. (Wick hadn't been cleaned for over a week when the Perrys arrived.) – and dirty stove oil.

Will char wick, install new gasket (meant for pickup truck caps) and fill can with pure kerosene. If that doesn't make ice cubes for my evening martini, I've wrecked the fridge by applying sledgehammer to warped bottom in attempt to lower burner so that new glass chimney would fit.

I'll tick off the tasks as completed. But every day I get sidetracked by ones that aren't on the list.

September 2, continued

Dark at 9 P.M. Sensational half-moon sky in cloud bank scrolled like a bedstead top. Sea lit up below. Big Dipper still hangs over house. Went out to see if it had begun to set.

Spent *entire* frigging day on fridge, but now she has a new gasket, three layers thick in places, charred wick, clean flue and pan filled with *kerosene* – (From now on!) Spoiled food tossed out.

Stranded bank tellers and Shelburne furniture salesman came by for a radio call. Strong NW wind kept them here. They left at sunset, and two outboards came looking for them afterwards –

(Offered them warm beer. No takers.)

September 3 (A.M.)

Ice! Blue flame. I turned it *down*. But now she [refridgerator] leaks again. Cleaning out the pan probably unplugged some holes of old gunk. Maybe I can control it with paper towel. If not, ashore to tinsmith along with boiler lid when I go back to NY.

Cellar door rot. Must go to work on this (and it's not even on the list) before tomorrow's rain. First rain in weeks is due. Sheep walk postponed?

Timmy just presented another baron of chipmunk. This one I'll freeze toward a full meal.

(P.M.) Cantaloupe slice of sky under rain clouds after sunset. Pitch black before 9 P.M. Labour Day, and I laboured on cellar door (somebody's favourite word) stained over black paint remaining and it seemed to take. Made a small contribution toward yard chair improvement (lined up pinned material for sewing machine, once it's readied) and washed the "annex" windows. They were hideous. Guess I'll go all the way around. If you're going to live year-round in a house it should have nice, clean windows, n'est-ce pas?

Surveyed the wood situation. Lifted logs from the ground where ants were busy devouring. Enough below for two winters' wood, or three – all cut to stove length, and a lot of it going to ruin.

The *Molly* seems to be leaking. Water aboard and no rain. Maybe moving the stove in strong wind split a seam. N Westerly took my dinner. Lid gone from box [small box for holding live lobsters], found upside down off transom.

Hadn't pegged them – so there are two biggies who'll find their way back to me. Rowed along the shore to retrieve the lid. Never saw it until I walked down to just the spot I thought it would have washed up. Will have to make broader buttons.

Wheeled another load of eelgrass to the "jardin." So it's chipmunk stew for supper.

September 4

Could have gone on eating my first caught mackerel all night. Lost a whopper, who snapped 100 yards of line off, leader and new lure – poor bastard, but he'll soon be tangled in a nearby net.

Visited the Sandy Point guys at last. Kisses and hugs all around. Said I thought it fitting to be saying hello the day after Labour Day. (To think I'd be in a faculty meeting somewhere now. No more ready to start a school year than I was in July.) Budd (Walter) Hemeon, 80 now, in green trousers with the fly sewn up. He stitched it himself this morning when he discovered the broken zipper. Ernest Goodick introduced me as a deer hunter to a fly fisherman who'd read Dad's books [*Upstream and Down*; *Big Stony*; *Anchorage Northeast*; *Our Native Inheritance: The Story of Corn in North America*] – Told me my beautiful deer is a lot more beautiful strung up from a tree. (She was back again, mid-afternoon.)

Nothing accomplished but faulty stove measurements and daydreams.

September 7

Heard Rampal flute sonata on Marine Band with button set to local (less power) until 1 A.M. Cold night – down to 4C, but warm inside. Discovered you get more heat, obviously, from Prizer Regal when there are no big pots (boiler, for instance) on hot spots. (Also learned to broil through side coal door – no smoke, no grease – closer to coals.)

Spent Wednesday in town. Highway engineer "couldn't promise" but would see what he could do for our "abandoned road." I repeatedly objected to the designation – saying their neglect had forced us to abandon it. – Stovepipes. Look into insulation, etc. Returned to exquisite sunset, copper and brass – and celebrated Howie's good news (taking courses in acting and jazz at Suny Purchase; living in Nyack with "concerned" people) with too much rum and Coca-Cola. Decided nix for a while.

Yesterday, dug out the "old spring" off the landing path and found orange clay. No water, but what seems to make one big crock of a hole deep in beside a chiselled boulder. Does it hold rainwater? – or did the old fellers use it to hold ice and preserve meat? Winter will tell. Fabulous sunset last night – clouds painted all colours and teal blue sky behind. Sun lowering to the south. Need only step out side door to see it. Golden slants across the orchard and meadow are dazzling. Set at 7:45. Front well *dry*. Cleaned out muck. (Margin Note: Sheep walk to Indian Point. Picked mint and an orange russula [mushroom] I won't eat again.)

North breeze today, bright sky and water. I'm out in a yard chair, topless. Must write letters before going ashore, for final stovepipe reducer. Then test the Franklin! Another cold night expected.

September 8

Came bare-assed up the landing path under a wintry moon last night. Put Stedmans' "on-special" Timex watch, "water-resistant," to the test a second time as I fell in deep off the poles trying to lug a mound of insulation from the *Molly*. No stovepipes ready. Instead of pricing Wilson's insulation first, I went to Woodworker's for price and succumbed again to the charms of the fellow in back – so three huge sacks of cotton candy were mounted to rooftop, more inside, and after laundromat I met the high tide in Carleton Village.

Herring/Mackerel nets are right in my compass course now, off the house.

Moon rose well south of privy; landing path black until wheelbarrow reached the meadow. I left *Molly* high on the skids so I can assess newly sprung leak (from transporting Franklin) and do some painting between high tides. Was going to clean lower orchard spring/well(?) and take sheep walk this weekend. As usual, other pressing priority intervenes. Never did get those letters written.

Young tinsmith maintains he stayed up till 4 A.M. and never turned on his heat Thursday night.

Dreamed of getting Bob Crofts to lasso the unshorn sheep and ram lambs at the light. Not a bad idea, as he was a rodeo star in his youth. My former school-paper anxieties have transferred to sheep, apparently. Is it "lasso" or "lassoo"?

Walter Perry thinks vitamin E "makes you sexy" and was surprised J & H [Joanna, sometimes referred to as Joge, and Howard] could have a stepmother when I'm still alive.

Just refilled the fridge with kerosene. First 20-litre can emptied. At this rate it will cost me $7 a week for icebox only – when I started here (or I guess when I first shifted the fridge to stove oil) total utility bill was 50 cents a week.

Saturday P.M.

Bushed. Minard's Liniment to shoulder. Too windy to paint the *Molly*. Spent day lugging insulation to upstairs, splitting big wood with maul and sledge, and starting on the lower orchard well (?) – stone work two rings thick – and deeper than I thought it went. Scooping muck with a trowel – about 6 inches left to scoop if it's a stone-ringed spring. If it's a well, I'll come to dumped stones. Some large boxes removed. Will tie a rope around me and go to it in an old bathing suit tomorrow, if it's warm enough.

Sky cantaloupe, deepening to persimmon, over cobalt water. The colours of Joanna's galaxy. [Joanna painted the 10,000-foot canvas *Self-Organizing Galaxy* on the rooftop of 5 World Trade Center in New York.]

September 9

Day begins with skinning a rabbit. Timmy left one leg, the back, and an enormous sack of guts for me. The old ewes are pacing around without their lambs, watchful, seem to be waiting for them to come back. Have they allowed them to go off on their own for the first time?

It *is* a spring! Reached bottom after sunset. (4 ft. down) Water pouring in. The surrounding land laid waste with pig poop, old bones, stones and waterlogged wood.

September 10

Scrubbed rocks, bailed spring again, and scattered lime. Got down to bottom of front well again and trowelled muck. Can't bend over, it's so narrow. How did the men build it? Small men? Man? Got hacking on dead stuff off the landing path. Spent rest of day hacking and dragging. Huge brush pile on the shore and more up here. Many nice places for the sheep now. I was so snarled and scratched, I would have frightened any visitors away, but haven't had any for three days.

September 12

"Take it out and sink it" seems to be the common remedy, cure-all, for whatever has caused a pastle [passel] of trouble. Now I know why the man who bought that cute baroque stove with so many enamel fittings and possibilities (but a badly rusted warped surface) actually took it out into West Green Harbour and dumped it. "I'd take these out to the harbour and dump them," was Bradford Perry's (when I finally *found* B. Perry's house) advice for my two inoperative bow saw blades. He and his wife are so familiar to me. He remembers me from Carleton Village crossing-days, but maybe he's my old feller? He put Dad's chock in his vice and wangled out the two, long, galvanized screws. I left the Perrys two lovely red pears from IGA. (They live on the Roseway River and remember when salmon were caught in front of their house.)

September 14

Hooked up the Franklin. Smoked like crazy when I started the fire, but closed the door and, once going, she did beautifully. Open log fire all afternoon during a windy SW rain. Even heated tea kettles. Tried all variations: w/ screen; doors closed; open fire which gave a tremendous heat. Never stoked it full, with doors closed, because the temporary mat underneath was already scorching. Put a pan with water under the firebox. Can't get more fireproof than that. Am so excited to have an open log fire and to be able to burn the cords of wood around here.

Went to check the spring (bailed out again yesterday) (3/4 full again) as the sun broke through cloud banks on its way to setting. Some apples are enormous. Lady Fair [a doe] appeared and came toward me as I talked to her, then flicked her tail and pranced away. She's around at all times of day now, in all places – I think there might be several Lady Fairs.

Sheep walk yesterday. Nearly ten miles. The old dame I saved near Sloop Rock was there again and seemed to know me.

Rediscovered the old lightkeeper's road to his house and landing. Eager to return. Darkness fell. Stray sheep and lamb turned mountain goat. If a ram, how will we catch him?

Started on kitchen flue covering. Have to rip the finish out in A.M. (After gathering wood before next storm and bailing *Molly*) and reset in position. Have nightmares of entire flue collapsing downward. (rotten cupboard studs?)

Last blow took down a big pear limb (one the hammock tied on to). Am checking large apples. Please do not wind fall.

September 17

Sun set at 7:30 last night through the front apple within sight of kitchen window. Heavy rain but no gale winds with storm (remnants of "Diana"). Enjoyed the Franklin. Sit and gaze into the fire, all the living room lamps lit and feel as though impossible dreams have come true. Rearranged the living room after The Evening Star retired upstairs. More spacious. The organ no longer looms as oversized and dominating the room. Maybe likewise Wilber will begin to withdraw from his dominant place in my psyche.

A small easy chair is needed.

Carpentry instructor Brian Race and his wife [Rilla] here Sunday. Measured for, and will do, four wood-frame storms for the kitchen. Also assessed the flue cabinet supports which I've left exposed in their bend to the left and worrying me. He'll return (but not for a while) with braces and clamps. Brought word that J's [Joanna's] painting will be finished Oct 2. Am planning to leave the 28th, next Friday. Poor cats. Will have to provide decent shelter somehow.

To everyone who asks about the place, I speak of 1960 and the years following as though they were only down the line a few years ... and realize later I'm speaking of years that sometimes predate the listener's birth. People must think I'm ancient, as well as odd.

Tired today. Can't seem to get started. Apples to pick. Dead wood in the meadows calling. Bonfire on the shore tonight? Will put up carrots in sand.

Fixed lawn mower. Then hit a rock. Flooded? $75 wrench set won't loosen blade.

Picked lovely big apples by the basketful, using my shirt as a receptacle up in the trees. Same shirt, I think, Joanna once put to same use. Had bonfire. Began dragging out old dead trees, left there by Howie's view clearing, at shoreline. Added some to bonfire, but too big a job for me. Got lost in blackness with wheelbarrow load of eelgrass. Timmy guided my feet homeward. Will have to seek out wheelbarrow in daylight.

September 19

Two large antlered bucks, one still bigger than the other, stood in the front yard and looked at me (in the window) a full minute before they turned and carried their antlers high into the swampy clearing and on to the lower orchard. Sensational day. Once again stripped bare at wood splitting. Worked on lawn mower but had to give up, unable to figure out how to lift top section off. Must return to A&B [Atkinson & Bower, a machine shop in Shelburne] for more free advice.

Continued the ever-enlarging job of clearing dead wood. Am now inching up either side of the meadow path. Made a brush fence back in the woods off the lower path to keep sheep from running in there on a gather.

Front spring well is full! (Barely a pail's worth in front well. Still using back well.) Rain barrel shower. NOT many more days when shower room will be warm enough. Will bank shed with eelgrass and spruce boughs. That might help.

Apple picking begins. Little tree in front ripens soonest. Have been dropping for a week. Sweet and delectable raw and cooked briefly with a little maple sugar. Peppering on skins doesn't affect the fruit (Not worms, as I thought) – but every one that falls is bruised. Picked some *big* green apples from lower orchard. Not ripe but the deer are biting into them. Into cellar bins.

September 22

Home after dark with a heap of damp laundry (after 5 quarters worth in the dryer on which was scratched "Aubrey H. Ripoff"), assorted baggage and 20-litre drums of kerosene. About 40 degrees. Am coming to realize I'm more than a little bit different. High tide in my favour and the stars were bright. Timmy and Annabelle had been shut in the house, so no guides for the blackened path. Wheelbarrow departs with load into uncharted regions.

No ice in fridge, and I've done everything right for it although flame was slightly roaring. Think it's the cold weather.

Sat admiring Franklin's fire, all downstairs lamps lit, my children's photos in their new Stedmans gold-metal frames (on special) on the pump organ, and flute on WQXR. [New York's Classical Music radio station. WQXR had both an FM and an AM station, "The Stereo Station of The New York Times," according to a 1986 ad.] Read letter from Tony. He's doing/planning the same for his island winter as I'm doing here.

Left Joanna's front page *Journal News* spread with Joan King. [An article in the Rockland County *Journal News*, New York, about Joanna's art installation on the roof of 5 World Trade Center.] Can children inherit a need to understand "What the hell is the meaning of life?"

September 24

Soaking both feet in boric acid out in the sun after fetching up a couple of big rusty nails at the front well. On daily inspection I digressed to pull up an old discarded well cover as well as carrying daily two logs for splitting, and have concluded that not only is the front well a snare and a delusion (still baked dry; maybe removal of overhanging trees is responsible, as Dad forewarned) but also our past practice of tossing "aside" the hacked, dead and replaced. Am paying for it now, in more than labour.

Over 80F! So I'm stripped bare again of course, while feet take in boric acid solution.

Made several jars of apple/green tomato & pepper/ raisin & currants chutney this A.M. which began cool and cloudy. All kitchen windows and doors now open. What a wonder the climate is here! Meanwhile, ostrich fern-like turkey feathers in the swamp clearing below, or like a child's Indian head-dress bought at a carnival.

I *still* haven't cleared the surrounding meadow of dead bay, etc. Soon the leaves will drop from the living. Yesterday Bob Croft and John [the assistant lightkeeper] arrived (long expected after Croft's vacation) and I elicited their help with a few light things, such as floor guards under the Franklin's legs and pulling apart the Evening Star's pipes. This expanded to an offer from Bob "to come down someday" and build me a flue (for the annex) with the bricks from the Rennehan house [an abandoned property, formerly the McNutt's Island Hotel] if I'd be ready with cement mix, "metal" and beach gravel.

Then he asked if I had a chainsaw, after I showed him and John the spring and mentioned how the big fallen spruce, from storm several years ago, bothered me so much. In 15 minutes he had most of one of them cut up in stove lengths, one of the three trees (I want down) to left of path felled, other boughs cut to clear where I didn't necessarily want cleared, and John had hauled all aside. I arrived with gloves and scarf, gung-ho to assist and directed John to stack dead boughs one place, green another, thick ends in direction of bow saw cutting, and in rather a flash a lot was done. Bob says he'll be down another day "to clean up" the tree he felled and "get the other two."

September 26

Yesterday was largely a bust although I hadn't much choice but to go ashore for tetanus shot. Right foot very bad. At the car I commented to myself that one of these days I would arrive at the car without my car keys, and soon found my purse, briefcase, tote bag and pockets to be empty of same. A summery heat wave, mist on the water and balmy wind accompanied me back to the *Molly* where I found keys in plaid jacket I brought along on the chance I'd return after dark. Otherwise, back to the island, tetanus incubating. (Margin Note: Happily, I hadn't hauled the punt up!) Stopped at Mrs. [Ruth] Van's with chutney and was given squash pie and tea. Mrs. Van says Tanya thinks her mother's camp days are over. New food processor and microwave oven; both of which I have no wish for, but someday, like the dishwasher, I might be given one or the other and never want to be without it (like the toaster oven). On the other hand, I might live without electricity for the rest of time, renting the J.B. [Jordan Bay] house and the V.C. [Valley Cottage] house for income. Except for Phil Scott's windmill.

Got the tetanus shot without feeling it, gave the new *Coast Guard* editor Joanna's story, and he, like every attractive young man here, wants to meet her. No ready-mix cement at Wilson's; new copper lid for boiler at tinsmith's: $49.49! (But it fits tight and keeps water hot overnight); no word from appraisers at Don Harding's; no mail at the P.O.; forgot to stop for Woodworker's potatoes special – on to Barrington where the sewing-machine yard-sale woman was not home with her extra bobbins, where Phil Scott was out in the woods for the day, a lot of work to do, said Fred, and wouldn't be back till dark; where Wilson's had no foam I could afford for the beds; where Mr. Surrette of the Trask Agency, who hasn't yet appraised the house, was in his *Shelburne* office, and where Arthur Weeks was found to be dead four years, his little shop turned into tacky Tudor apartments.

Depressed, I pulled off Route 3 at Clyde River and fortunately found Mr. Stoddard stone deaf but still alive (the epileptic antique/junk dealer who calls me "dear girl") so mood was somewhat uplifted. No chair for living room though we visited a pleasant Perry who had a tacky chair for sale. People fishing for salmon on the Clyde. Drove round the peninsula to Carleton Village, fog and clouds, much colder, no one home at Skipper's so I left a long note and phoned Aunt Ellen! She had *not* received my massive letter and hence had had no word from me whatsoever since Dan's death. I must have mailed it two weeks ago. Parked the car at the water and sat there looking at the horn.

Spirits revived, as they always do, once safely home with the new boiler lid and polished boiler, which *leaked* but now seems to have patched itself. Calm seas, high tide, last night.

Today a howler. Marine forecast and reports only now, 4:30 P.M., admitting to winds over 30 knots. Expected to accomplish so much indoors today (the sewing machine still sits in the kitchen, uncleaned, unoiled!) but the morning went on the lamps and fridge, which had an unaccountably crusted wick which may explain malfunction, dishes (piled from two days), spring and well water, eelgrass and oil fill at the shore ... Does not justify the passage of time, but I'm half sick – actually have a sore jaw, and I think I would have had tetanus without the shot. Still limp. Made applesauce and talked to the sheep.

They all have names now: Heavenly Grace (my own ewe who has had so many surviving lambs); Helen, her yearling; Maude, her mother; Wanda, her two-year-old who escaped the shearing (her full name is Wanda Lust); Pauline, a stocky chiveat [Cheviot]; Diana, the fancy one who slants her eyes and points up her tail when she walks (so does her lamb!); and Kay, spelled Che (Guevara – full name), the dark, strong-willed Hispanic. Haven't named the six lambs, though I think Wanda's is June. Grace's deserves a particularly pretty name. Gazing into the Franklin again. Would write letters, but I seem to reach the people sooner than the mail does.

September 28

Forecast cloudy, but dazzling autumn day which I spent most of in town. Clouds and rain and heavy easterly coming so I plan to leave for N.Y. tomorrow on the high tide after establishing the cats in the old privy. Bob Croft will look in on them (probably *daily!*) (saw him in town) – Skipper met me at the landing, dazzling also in his blondness and smiles – Helped haul the *Wynken* into the fish house, and again was there to help at the dead low tide returning from Carleton Village.

Split wood right after breakfast, and either I'm getting stronger and more accurate then, or the cold in the wood assists me, or both, but they went like firecrackers.

Saw the Mounties to commence possession of Dad's revolver and ammunition – Found my driver's license gone – How long have I been driving without it?

Ordered a Sears special portable kerosene heater – For shower room, guest room, shed – but they're costly and so is the kerosene they guzzle at 6 litres per 17 hours. Got another 4 foot x 6 foot foam piece at People's to soften these beds. Need only chipboard between springs and mattresses for the two upstairs and this will rival the Hilton at Christmastime.

Am now a member of the Co-op – Bought some things to take home.

Bringing in the moss-strewn trap. New moon low? Exquisite sunset and evening sky. Must go down in the dark now to bring punt and trap up the rest of the way. May I return …

October 24

I did, a week ago from New York, from what seemed a space odyssey to "Windows On The World"'s "hors d'oeuvre room" [The Hors d'Oeuvrerie was a smaller eatery at the top of the North Tower of the World Trade Center, whereas Windows on the World was the main restaurant.] – Guy Tozzoli [director of the World Trade Department of the New York Port Authority, a key figure in the building of the Twin Towers, and founder of the World Trade Centers Association] was taught to pronounce it but not yet to spell it – after Joge's magnificent party and accolade and speech to all the flashing, reeling cameras, behind which I found myself planted in stupefied bemusement until somebody hauled me out to see and share … Above it was 2001 after McNutt's [a reference to the movie *2001: A Space Odyssey*].

Then house re-rented, marathon pack up and takeoff, proposal at bus stop included, Carlowe's Cabins in Wesley, Maine, for halfway point where Mac broke off the key in the lock at midnight ferry from St. John's after free ferry to Deer Island (we played tourist on gained time – gained an hour while we *killed* time), Sandy Point in pre-dawn, men shoved in the *Molly*, out to the island with carload including Christmas ornaments and pick-axe – CAR IS ENTERED on residence (*returning*) at last – Felt I was truly "returning resident." Don't think I leave again for more than three months ever.

Arrived at island ablaze with crimson alders (lamb kill? wild pear?) (Margin Note: *must research*) birch still golden but apples gone, sheep gone, cats gone. Warm and *gorgeous* but lifeless. Worried. If my precious daughter weren't with me, I would have felt sick with loneliness.

Annabelle returned crying all the way to kitchen window next morning after J's jog. Timmy came back days later (A. purring loud enough to hear at the light meanwhile) and sheep ambled in, *all of them*, soon after.

11:10 P.M.

Alone again. Skipper whisked Joanna off from laundromat to meet 4 P.M. plane. No time to grieve. We had a real *vacation* together. Cleared more of wilderness path to NE bluff. Found our 2-year-old trail still *legible*. Caught restobols ["restobols" was Joanna's attempt to spell "lobsters" backwards] sretsbol (she had it wrong!) chopped wood, sunbathed, enjoyed the Franklin – (for hours!) and each other's company. I love my daughter.

New kerosene heater works fast. I'm sure Mom and Dad would have ordered me one of these if they'd been around. Good for guest room, shower and upstairs. Croft is threatening to build flue with bricks from Rennehan house, but now that J's gone, maybe he won't.

Brian Race has made storms for kitchen. Due here Sunday. 12 N

Phil Scott didn't answer phone.

Hunters at C.V. [Carleton Village] wharf tonight. No signs of poaching. All ducks. Lyndon helped load boat. Came over with Dad's 32 c. in briefcase. Permit to transport until dark. Sundown soon after 6 P.M. *Dark* coming up path. Both cats waiting at landing.

Lobster cooking. Tomorrow wild sheep walk with new binoculars. Ram at light, reported, next day, opening day of deer season. *Must be here.* Have not seen young ram though Crofts says he's been here. Nor bucks. Have seen two does since return. But not as before. Will save, if possible. As well as sheep.

Why does it happen that when I come home alone at dark and cook supper it's after 1:30 A.M. when I go to bed? (Check handwriting for clue to answer)

October 26 FIRST DAY OF DEER SEASON

I can see how the time will go this winter.

Spent *whole day* frigging with lamps and wood stoves. Still haven't unpacked paper stuff or balanced bank-books. Entertained five from the Cape Island camp tonight. They are all ages, and charmers, every one. Assured me they wouldn't shoot a deer on this place, nor a young one anywhere. We talked island history, paths and roads and fields. Our ten-acre piece across the road is "the old pasture."

"Russell Hemeon's boy" dragged out a bagged twelve-point buck from the north field at dawn today. Story has it he had no license but was with a girl who had one. (There goes my biggest, I guess.)

Sheep walk yesterday turned up *two* rams raring to go. – One on [land] grant 20's hill among ewes; another northeast of light with a small flock, some unshorn. I followed them back in over the cliffs and barrens. Must capture them or all is lost. Sent walkie-talkie message at night, picked up by camp and relayed ashore. I finally spoke to Barry Crowell who called Cliff V.B. [VanBuskirk] for me, and Cliff arrived today at the landing, all dressed in orange-red, saying the fools hunting on the island will shoot at anything. He came with Tasha [his sheepdog] and binoculars, but hearing my description of rams and whereabouts, turned back to phone the Perrys. Hope to hell they get here by Sunday. There goes my time with the carpenter if they do.

Tomorrow I'll have a 3-wheeler and cart to use whenever I want!

October 27

A concession to the modern age: 3-wheeled Honda and cart are now parked facing the shed doors. Will I drive them?

Return to Standard Time. (Atlantic)

October 28

Brian Race and wife [Rilla] due at noon, C.V. [Carleton Village] wharf, but winds are due to build to 20+ SW. With fog and "drizzle." Also a chance that Perrys will arrive to round up rams. After a day of wood splitting and hauling, I went to start the 3-wheeler and couldn't raise a spark.

Something not turned on, I guess. So many switches I was told about so quickly.

Lyndon arrived in 4-wheeler (before I couldn't start mine) and asked if he could "park it" here now that the Cape Islanders had left. "I'm gonna have a garage," I said. Was reluctant to say yes but it would only be for a week, he said, and he's done me several favours. "Sure, Lyndon, you can keep it here behind the shed," I said. "I just don't like the noise, but maybe it will scare the deer from here –" I shouldn't have let on that there were deer here. If the deer *stayed* here, they'd still be alive, but I'm sure someone has taken my tame doe now, and my spirit sinks at the thought.

Lyndon was going to help me move a rock or two to make a road behind the barn, but he took off "to leave some apples" somewhere; I heard two shots seeming to come from up on the high road, and he never came back. Either he is a victim of a hunting accident or he has taken my big cinnamon Lady Fair. Second possibility more likely than first. Christ, maybe he only wounded her and followed her till he lost her. These are thoughts to unsettle my serenity. Hurry end of deer season!

Crofts arrived on his 3-wheeler, all dressed in khaki, Barny Rudge [Barney Rubble] at the wheel, ([Fred] Flintstone's friend), and when I repeated Cliff's assessment of the hunters on the island, that they would shoot at anything that moved, he shrugged: "Then they'll shoot me. Nobody'll miss me anyway." Said he was sorry he'd "made [me] mad yesterday," arm around me, and I didn't comment. (Not allowing me up the light when I had walked all the way there with binoculars for that express purpose after telling him earlier it was what I wanted to do.) Then he said he'd go to town and "get [his] money back" for the chain he got for the camp's 3-wheeler now that they were storing it here. Later turned out he had ordered it, not paid for it, and I wonder if he had even done that. I offered to buy it from him, and I'll bet I never see it. He now says the flue can't be moved, and has not mentioned returning to his woodcutting, so I can't figure the guy out.

A knock at the door. *Ron Perry!* Fortunately I'd gotten up after (or before) writing the above to gain the extra hour on the waking side, not the sleeping, and at 7 A.M. (A.S.T.) was filling, lighting and loading the fridge, emptied ashes, started fire and had washed sleeves of bathrobe (kerosene on elbows) when Ron caught me sweeping dust heap in middle of kitchen floor in nightgown and plaid flannel shirt.

Took two bananas, a granola for breakfast – off to light. Van, Cliff, Dwight and Ron's Marc all here. They'd come without key to truck and had to go back. That's happened before: thus Ron had a little time at the house to view it and my 13 sheep. Driving to light I told Van about Crofts and the chain (getting his "money back") – and Van said not to believe what he says. He had Van empty a freezer because the Dept. [Department of Fisheries and Oceans] was taking it, and the freezer is still there. (That among many other things.) Had him clean out the "oil house" and now keeps his horse there.

A botched gather at the light. Was telling Van that Crofts cracked Howard up as Barny [Barney], Flintstone's friend, when the sheep came at us on the sea cliffs, and we lost several in the helter-skelter. Cornered a bunch and pulled out two ram lambs and one unsuccessfully operated on. Let the rest go. Four unshorn ewes. I may have mistaken a ram lamb for ram there – but was sure of the big snozzoler up on the south hill so on we went, and praise God we got him – along with a couple more ram lambs. *Still* missing rams, but they *must* be dead.

Mac and I blocked a break, fallen behind the rest, so we weren't useless.

We all inspected a drowned bear on the beach, lying splay-legged on the remnants of its back. Filled with maggots, shot with holes. Dwight inspected its teeth – said he "had a birthday yesterday" – and pulled a bone out from under – said "there's his horn" –

I love these Vans so – and Ron Perry, for that matter – could live out my life with the likes of them.

Never had to race to the Races in a 20-knot southwestern. Cliff had phoned to tell them I'd be occupied. (Thanks to walkie-talkie!) Couldn't come for another two weeks, Brian said.

Wind is piling in the front door tonight, but warmer. I'm discovering the leaky spots, at any rate.

October 29

Am running an orphanage here. Four small homeless lambs have joined my own – 3 runty wethers and a ewe, scraggly and unpretty; I guess their mothers don't care enough to come looking for them, separated by yesterday's ram gather. Looked out the window at 7 A.M. to a young deer, but grayer than my tame one. Then saw two does and two *small* young ones (no more spots) in the orchard. Lord protect them all.

Daylight shortened now to such a degree I must *accomplish* during the few hours of visibility without lamps. At least I get up earlier because of standard time. Begins to get light at quarter to seven, instead of eight, so I get up then. Dark by 5:30, which will greatly diminish my time ashore. Must get started earlier!

Whole bunch of sheep at the end of the bar. Looking for lambs that are here?

Have decided I'll not be a dirty old hermit except when working outside. Had on smudged sweatshirt for a day of mild indoor action, and changed to clean sweater. Wear earrings and lipstick too. You never know ... but of course when Ron comes knocking at the door I'm caught in long peach gown under red-checked, ragged flannel shirt five sizes too large. Think I should also try talking less to myself aloud. Quite embarrassing when one gets caught.

Mrs. Hyde's Hostelry in full swing this afternoon. Lambs without mamas all over the place, wandered in from yesterday's ram gather, and *one* outside ewe who is, of all people, my old long-tailed ewe from down south – one of my first "grazing fees" that has built my flock. Hope she stays so I can look after her this winter. She has a part Suffolk lamb, a good one, which means she was in the vicinity last year at breeding season. DEER all over the place, including a doe with *twins,* but no sign of my Lady Fair and the comical young one, both victims of poachers' guns while I was away, undoubtedly.

October 30

Watching a golden, almost-half-moon lower to the sea and listening to WQXR thanking Payne Webber [the financial services company that sponsored the program]. Learned to start the 3-wheeler today with John and Crofts' help (Crofts brought a load of manure) and drove it on my own after breaking a road through where Lyndon had suggested and vanished. Moved a *large* stone with pick-axe and lead pipe, thanks to watching Francy deal with similar challenges years back and again this summer at the orchard wall where some rocks had fallen.

Maude's son is stirring up trouble, humping (attempting to) Helen, and sniffing out some of the other ewes. Something hangs low, but I'd thought all along he was fixed. Followed them close enough to lasso, so I'll have to make me a (lariat? caviat?) tomorrow.

October 31

Spent Halloween friggin' with the lawn mower. Gary Butler's instructions [Gary was a mechanic at Atkinson & Bower machine shop] were for some other B & S [Briggs & Stratton] wheel but I didn't realize this until I'd smashed off a fin that holds a basket screw and had driven a rectangular hole through the base of a (drawing) that I was supposed to "bang counterclockwise." Got the blasted nut off by horse-sense method of extending the ratchet handle with a five-foot lead pipe. Speaking of horses, I began spreading Crofts' manure on the "garden" on top of composting grass clippings and stove ash. Sun set on my labours – gorgeous sunset – at 5:10 P.M. (!) and I hadn't carved the Jack-O-Lantern of my 99 c. pumpkin from Woodworkers. Decided not to agonize over said neglect, for doubtless no one would come to see it anyway, and I'd have a pumpkin for pie. Doe and twins here again, morning and evening.

November 1

No one did come. Cape Islanders not here yet, but Crofts and John arrived to see the "garden" progressing and have coffee. Told me "the kids" had better Halloween costumes this year than ever, but they couldn't come down as the jeep had no headlights. (No lights "allowed" by the Department of Transportation because they're not supposed to operate boat at night!!) I asked who had seen the costumes. Bob said John had. Those kids study by correspondence course and never, so far as I can tell, see other people, their own age or otherwise.

Covered whole garden with h.s. [horse manure]. Now think I should start another section with Sears tarp and cover this with eelgrass and spruce boughs. Fence an area 4x the cultivated space next spring. Who's the big garden for?

Little Man gives a stormy blow for tomorrow, but can't put off going ashore any longer.

Storm doors are scrubbed in bleach and airing. I now seem to split wood till noon every cold morning. Made gimcrack well cover of old door for new water source (lower orchard spring). Ram/wether lamb seems to be minding own business today.

Several deer this morning. Hunter on trail late afternoon, eyeing our orchards long and hard as he walked by. Timmy was off on high road, spotted at light by Crofts, but when a shot sounded off in that direction, I wondered if he'd get home for supper. He did, an hour late.

Enjoyed heated shower room tonight. (Will make insulated pad for shower floor.) Washed hair before trip ashore. Don't like smelly hermits.

Dog food can smashed large bottle of 7-Seasons Italian dressing all over pantry, bought with "double coupon and special" and never needed anyway. Full of carcinogens. Now I've a mess to clean up.

November 4

First day in many that I've seen no one else. Was expecting Cliff all afternoon to come and attempt to catch the ram at the light, but fortunately didn't expect him too hard. So I've painted first coat on one side of both storm doors, and taken apart lawn mower once again, this time with really broken flywheel pin – will take gouged wheel into Gary Butler. Split wood most of morning, sonofabitch wood and for the most part worthless, but went doggedly on gathering more of the same to finish off 2nd pile by front well and Crofts sawed up the dead tree. Front well still dry; new spring almost full!

Sheep are suddenly dropping enormous turds around the place, which I gathered. Assessed front scraping and mildew job – *so much* to do before winter, am afraid I'll get caught unready. Continue to be partway into a score of tasks or haven't even begun some, such as insulation and sewing machine which still sits in the middle of the kitchen floor.

Letters to write! A day's worth, at least, of business mail and postcards. Had such a loving message from Joge. I basked in it returning home last night by 2C moonlight. Overstayed in town at Joan's. Sun sets at 5:05 and sky is dark by 6.

The apple tree in front was filled with a variety of birds this morning, all after something where the apples had fallen. A yellow-green-chartreuse-rose breasted bird I'll have to look up. Bigger than a warbler.

The bushes in front are suddenly giving out bright red berries. So lovely, and a dazzling day, but no deer sighted. My Cape Island friends took two does this time. I bleed with them. Disturbing thoughts today of living with the dead.

Prizer Regal now *loads from the front*, thanks to Friday's courageous go-at-it again. Just tried harder than the last time, and up came the iron plate. Oven lining now busted in several places, patched with "stove cement," and weighed down by old flat iron. Did *not* get ashore Friday. Gale winds gusting to 50+ knots. Blew like hell. Went Saturday, did heaps of laundry, but missed stove oil and am almost out.

Aladdin lamp is working properly at last. Will probably use it a lot for quick heat and bright work light this winter. Will have to get some work done after dark, because there is so much dark.

Keep dreaming about houses I've neglected.

Still houseflies buzzing and scaring Mac from room to room. Still heaps to sweep. One season I won't feel sorry to see go is housefly season.

November 10

Blanket of frost on the roof, on grass, this morning, not for first time, but thicker than the usual. House like a Christmas card. Admiring this I slipped and fell en route to the privy. Frost can be very slippery, I discovered at boat landing yesterday morning. Privy hole, however, not the icy contact I had anticipated. Wood seems to chill less, or to take on body heat enough to make sitting a while bearable. Mist rising across harbour in high cloud over one stretch of beach and no other.

Two trips ashore this week. Before yesterday's I split four or five logs with 25 F into them, and found the going a lot easier. Excellent before-breakfast exercise, which I mentioned to the post office lady but I don't think she appreciated hearing about my "building up a sweat." I forgot that women "perspire." Have spent an inordinate amount of time looking for hiking boots, lightweight and waterproof. Settled for snow joggers. At least they are warm and seem to fit.

All tasks take longer than time allotted for them. (This has been keeping me from sleeping well.) Garden still needs one more wheelbarrow load of eelgrass. (I must have brought up over 50 for house and garden; house still needs more.) Then spruce boughs over that. Guess I'll use the 3-wheeler and cart. Will try to work out a logging road to the lower orchard. Have doubled the future garden's size with the tarp. Now must spread sheep drops, horse manure and stove ash under that, and spruce boughs over it, to hold down tears and block out light. *If* I can get mower working again I'll add some hay to top as before.

Then must dig dooryard garden and plant bulbs.

Storm doors almost ready. 2nd coat on one side to go. Did a lot of puttying.

Haven't begun insulation job or sewing machine. Rain coming, but so many troublesome letters to write. EBW's [Ernest Beverly Walden, Elizabeth's brother and only sibling] lawyer in Liverpool will require several hours, but I've no time to go over there. Sun sets at 5 P.M.

Sent S.O.S to Amos and note to Phil. Van and Cliff due daytime for another attempt to catch ram at light. Brian Race and wife not until the 18th now with storm windows.

I can see where people can become peculiar during long spells of isolation. Talking to oneself is, as Joanna says, only thinking out loud, but it's also to fill a human need for company. Had a fleeting moment at supper table last night that made me collapse head into hands in fit of meaninglessness. But I think that could have happened in Valley Cottage as well. Akin to fear of death.

Only the blue jays are coming to the food I've put out. Sheep have departed, I hope only temporarily. Doe and twins still visit, despite rampant hunting. Lord protect her. Already I'm losing sleep over the sheep. Thought Che (Kay) had been shot by a hunter because I hadn't seen her for several days. Stayed awake half one night over this, but she's alive and well, headstrong as ever, marching off to her own beat and the devil take the hindmost. (What does that saying mean? "The devil's advocate" is mentioned at least once, every day on radio now. How like sheep – other than Kay – people are.)

Election results, [Ronald] Reagan's landslide and greatest electoral sweep in [U.S.] history, has me considering giving up my citizenship.

November 12

Balmy day, like early spring thaw – Blue Jays have figured out the seed bells, and went at them all day like kids at a swimming hole leaping for the swinging ring. Burned off the fuel gleaned from each seed in the effort of getting it.

Dug bulb bed length of guest room shed, south side and half of gable end outside kitchen window. Dug up many flat stones. Amos's drain? Or my flagstones 20 years back? Will have to move wagon wheels.

A pox on all machinery. Still can't start the 3-wheeler, nor can Crofts or John (here today struggling with it and picking apples). I had figured out a road to the lower orchard and was all set to get a cartload of spruce boughs for the vegetable garden when it wouldn't start. Finally got lawn mower going and it wouldn't stop! Am repairing flywheel with epoxy.

Elizabeth's "little red house" on McNutt's Island, 1966.

The *Molly* with Elizabeth at the tiller, Mary (Mac's mother), Howard in the centre, and Joanna in the cuddy.

Amos's Landing, where Elizabeth would land her boats. Her house is in the background on the left.

Amos's Landing, 1968. Howard is in the foreground and Joanna is near the water with one of the punts and the *Molly* behind her.

Launching the *Molly*.

Mac, Elizabeth's "white-haired boy."

Joanna and Ollie the Seagull.

Sheep at the front door checking out Elizabeth's hard-won and precious firewood.

Elizabeth and the Prizer Regal in the kitchen.

Howard and Elizabeth at the Shakespeare House, 1992.

Skipper at the helm of his boat.

Elizabeth's stone monument with the limestone squirrel from her mother's garden.

McNutt's Island Journal 2
November 14, 1984 – January 28, 1985

November 14

They're talking about the importance of computer know-how on WQXR, and here I sit by oil lamp. Might be using a seagull quill if Peoples hadn't put a special on ball points. NW gale forecast for tonight, and I hear the wind building now, although the barometer is rising. Did not move the *Molly*. Decided she was better off here at the mooring than the head of the cove at anchor. Tomorrow will tell. (First time a gale has been forecast, although we've certainly had gale winds before this.)

Yesterday I actually completed a scheduled, difficult task. Dug flower beds, foot deep or more all turned and sifted – beautiful earth – felt Mom's spirit inhabiting me as I fell to my knees and worked – along both south ends of house – wider off kitchen so fence will match line up of guest wing fence (fence post and poles will be a winter activity, I guess). Added sand where needed (unearthed a flagstone walk under a foot of soil –) wood ash, compost, and scattered horse manure on top. (Hope that wasn't a mistake.) Then planted a hundred bulbs – red and yellow tulips, daffodils, grape hyacinths and crocus – and transplanted some uprooted narcissus. Covered it all with wood chip mulch. Might add some eelgrass, and hope to plant hyacinths if I can get some in town, and want delphiniums for the back row but haven't faintest idea when to plant it – in what form? – seed? bulb? tuber?

Took two days; first shifting wood chopping operations to shed and cleaning out much of the heap in center of shed. Room now for the Honda that still won't start. Waldo worked on it today with two of his pals. The others were back at the camp "unable to walk" because they'd eaten so much "cabbage stew for dinner." They didn't know about the gale, which seems odd.

Also moved all canned and liquid food from the pantry to kitchen, rearranging cupboard and installing a "provision" shelf behind door to living room. Cleaned out behind it so mop, ironing board and odd sacks don't confront you when door to living room is closed. Which is often now that I'm working outside all day. Don't bother to run the Franklin. Just keep kitchen and bedroom warm for the time I'm inside.

Climbed the birch by the road to bring down high broken branches for firewood, and noticed later how easily I had sprinted up there. Must be in pretty good shape.

Always too dog-tired at night, though, even to read.

November 15

Making the playhouse work is what's making me so happy.

Strong winds again today my excuse for not going ashore, and bright skies my excuse for not writing business letters. Cold though, but I've a new outfit: green sweatpants, gray sweatshirt, and Howie's old blue hooded sweatshirt overall, my new "snow joggers" from Stedmans $30 special. Ideal for wood splitting before breakfast, and comfy enough to stay in all day. The pounds are leaving my hips. (Margin Note: Cleared out connection way to make room for coats, boots, and box of hardwood separate from the rest.)

Waldo and party here off and on all day frigging with the Honda. Still doesn't go. Split pea soup is on the Franklin.

November 16

30 knot winds WSW – blasting through front door crack so I installed narrow foam weatherstrip and added paint to storm door which I had to bring inside out of wind. Seems to need five coats. Each time I had latex "2nd coat" it rains – *only* then, and only (on) the storm doors, it seems. Tulip beds are barely damp. Will have to make door knob. Near Gales forecast for tomorrow, and colder. And gales Sunday, so no storm windows or Brian Race to brace the kitchen flue, which has been periodically sending down a barrage of mortar powder – one such on my head as I bent over dustpan.

More than a week without mail, and it begins to tell. Too long out of touch. Tonight WQXR cut off, which isn't unusual, but then I couldn't get WCBS on AM or *any* New York station. [WCBS was an all-news station.] Heard only Puerto Rican and South American. Eerie, if not downright sinister, but my unsettled state was soon assuaged by Yarmouth's Country Music top ten on FM, complete with Shelburne tide schedule and marine weather.

No exercise today, but for grinding dry dog food into cat crumbles, having run out of dry cat. Swept another trillion flies upstairs in preparation, I hope, of installing stove and insulating.

November 17

Hints of what's to come. Freezing temp with 30-40-knot Westerly gale driving slush in its rain showers and wind through all the west window cracks. Finished, more or less, the front storm door in the guest room which I kept above

50F for the final paint, with the Aladdin lamp. Then scuffed the paint off wheelbarrowing to the front in the wind and having to bang the door in with board and back of hatchet because paint, putty and dampness had made it too big. A good tight fit, however, along with the weatherstripping, in this cold wind.

No chance to write letters or read. Spend entire evening stoking fires and trying to cook. Burnt right through all the wood in the house. A sampling of what's to come.

New York radio reception continues to be poor. All I hear from Boston is about bludgeoned and missing children and Saturday night murders of women picked up in bars. That and the traffic reports. A drawbridge out. And Baby Fay [Fae], of course, who died yesterday when her walnut-sized baboon heart stopped. Memorial for her today. What of the baboon whose heart stopped? Any words for him?

I am understanding, quite lucidly, more about myself and why I am here. Not that it's news. I've already written it out in two novels. I was right then, and see it even more clearly now. Then I had to write to discover. Now I can see without writing. And so I don't?? (Write ...)

November 18

Despite the wind and cold I connected with Brian, wife Rilla, and four storm windows, thank God, which he fitted on, then worked on collapsing chimney and also planed front storm door. Gave them each a house special afterwards (bourbon and Joanna's rosehip syrup and wine). Yesterday's gale pulled up landing center post. Privy door frozen shut this morning. Logs like splitting into stone. My shoulder is suffering the strains of survival.

Some lovely music on local FM. Bach flute concerto played by Rampal and now harpsichord. Very amusing veddy British old M.C., so who needs New York which continues to be phased out by weather or satellite or some other phenomenon.

Only 9:15 but I could go to sleep right now so I guess I will –

November 19

Very cold. Strong NW wind. Down to -6(C) tonight. I've frozen ice trays for the evening cocktail outside shed door. (Fridge is off, and keeps food cold.) Frustrated in two efforts today: cemented the broken stove lining from 6 A.M. to 8 A.M. today by lamplight and flashlight while the kerosene heater and Aladdin lamp warmed the kitchen. Thought I had a perfect fit. Then today's fires have burnt away the cement. Pieces remain, in place, at least. Then went to low tide landing, moved big boulders and banged away at center post, managing to lower it only a little and split it to pulp on top. Then banked the house with eelgrass and need ten more wheelbarrow loads to finish all the way around. Which it needs. Patched connection shed holes with chair foam that had washed up at the landing, nailed a piece of wood to the shed door frame to close a gap and cleaned out the shingle barrel. Stuffed old seat foam in the kitchen drain hole, filled the shower floor with insulation – washed the new storm windows (too cold to paint them) and put them back on one at a time. Moved some wood and sawed some small dead apple. Kept living room closed off to spare the Franklin pile. To bed at 9. (Margin Note: spectacular stars)

November 20

Must announce at 6:45 P.M. that the house is *warm.* 72F! This has been a real contest with "intense low pressure area *anchored* off Labrador" for too many days now bringing gales or gale warnings every day for two weeks. Still haven't gotten ashore for mail, groceries, laundry, oil, etc. but supplies are holding out. I barely keep up to date on the splitting and sawing, leaving little time for insulating and eelgrass banking.

Radio's "nightmares" of traffic jams make me feel fortunate to have my nightmares keeping me physically fit. Shoulder is sore, but Timmy sleeps square on it each night to keep it warm. Up at 5:30 in the mornings now, to warm the house. I've tried to cover Mac with "the old bathrobes" but he panics out of his sleep. He takes a long run somewhere before breakfast while I split wood, and that keeps him warmed up and from growing old.

Survival is all here. No time to work out tenant's deposit returns or letter to Liverpool lawyer re: J.B. [Jordan Bay house] inventory. They'll just have to wait.

Insulated inside cellar door, but east kitchen wall is still cold. (Eelgrass piled a foot high around cellar door.) I'll bet the window sills and frames need caulking.

November 24

Thursday ashore, the *only* day in two weeks without gale warnings or gales. Got back after dark, Skipper called, sat till 11 P.M. and this farmer didn't get to bed till after 2 A.M. and four Bloody Marys – Slept late Friday and have had to make up for it with the wood splitting, and moving, sawing and clearing and eelgrass banking.

Sailed to Sandy Point today beating into a 25-knot Northwester to meet Will Butler [another mechanic with Atkinson & Bower] scheduled to work on the 3-wheeler here. Spray in the face is a chilly proposition in late November. Mac hid in the bow. (We got hung up on a rock in the breaking waves trying to get off the landing.) Will couldn't come but *will* tomorrow, on his own steam. Saw the men at S.P. [Sandy Point] and they all grinned to see me sopped and surviving.

Thought, while I worked, of turns my life has taken and of my kids. Letters from both and packages reminding me my birthday is coming up. 51st. I cease to attempt to reckon the time. J. says H. is doing so well with his music and that Bob [Wilber] is "excited" to be working with him. If Howie pulls through this to be the musician I've always thought he could be, to have a happy, productive life, I'll be fulfilled. [Howard lived with a diagnosis of schizophrenia, though he and his family questioned this label. He was prescribed drugs that his mother believed were detrimental.] Nothing means more to me than that. Uncanny how Howie is like Bob in looks, manner and style. Hair, chin and stance. And now to be blooming with not only the sound but the freedom to go with it and send it soaring – My own son – How strange. How wonderful. That the chasm in my life should be filled this way.

New moon traced in the sunset tonight, and WQXR loud and clear again. Gone are the Puerto Ricans. Back comes New York. On a moonbeam?

Overheated the kitchen tonight! On punk wood, yet. Insulated its attic ceiling with R20 on Wednesday and washed my hair in two basins afterwards. (Too cold for the shower now, even with the heater.)

Timmy takes off for a couple of days at a time, now, now that he's taking my presence here for granted again. When he's gone Annabelle tries to keep my shoulder warm.

She has a deep gash on her nose.

November 25

(Caption under a sketch of *Molly*: "low tide at 5:30 from kitchen window. I drew the *Molly* right the first time, and then wrecked it with improvements. Thinking of so many romantic resolutions, when I can't even draw the boat, that will never be – but that's all right, so long as I can think about them. Don't ever attempt to improve on nature. I rarely do. Crescent moon and two stars over it were YELLOW and BIG as they sank toward black horizon at 6:30 P.M.")

No mechanic arrived. Expected him all day and so didn't go ashore to make Sunday phone calls and mail letters. Instead Crofts and John came, once for coffee and gave me a lesson in sharpening a chainsaw; again with a load of manure.

Was voyeur this morning while large buck courted lovely doe at the front well and chasing her all through clearing and about the lower orchard. Her small faun and last year's yearling looked on perplexed and occasionally got in the way. Crofts says bucks will gore the fauns if they get in the way, but this didn't happen, and I doubt much of what he says.

November 26

Field full of robins, and all the sheep and lambs loping back. Warmer but cloudy, so I overslept. Missed seeing the laden lobster boats steam out for first day of season – but will never forget that sparkling first morning in Jordan Bay as they raced out proudly to claim their bottom grounds.

Now I can open my presents!

All day long the boats came and went, steaming down heaped up and returning empty, so I didn't miss seeing decks piled high with traps. Alone all day on my birthday, but heart full of Joge and Howie, their dear presents and messages, the miracle of Howard's recovery, and the wonder of Joanna's love and liveliness. Her wagon full of groceries is the cutest miniature toy I've seen. I lingered a long while over every little bag and its contents, and the tool box with message inside. Wore Howie's pink shell necklace on my gray sweatshirt all day, and the twilight sky was pink and gray for the first time.

November 27

Sweetness and June are gone. Could hunters have actually shot them? Painted storm windows in diffused balmy light. First "mild" day in weeks. Lobster boats back and forth all day, lights on at twilight as the last came back. Felt as though I had loads of company as I lit up the kitchen.

Have been finally writing business letters, but have yet to deal with EBW's lawyer. Hangs over me like smog. Must get it behind me. Where are my lambs?

WQXR's Christmas ad for tickets to the Royal Shakespeare Companys *Cyrano de Bergerac* gave me a stab of homesickness, but the radiant silver sea and sky lingers with me long after twilight (though it's dark out the windows. *Nothing* out there when one leans to look for a cat or something.)

December 1

Last day of deer hunting. Expected rain and strong Westerly any minute so worked steadily after I lit the stove, on wood, eelgrass, storm windows (now with 2nd coat), caulking, bailing boat, finding ornaments – and *June* came home with Helen, and found Wanda at last. Rain didn't come until 4 P.M. Then I had breakfast.

December 2

– overslept. *Deer Season Over!!* Buck courting beautiful doe in the 9 A.M. sunlight – in the back orchard. Loaded camera too late. Did up a breakfast of fried banana, eggs and bacon, hot blueberry muffin, coffee and *fresh squeezed orange juice* – was admiring it as what Joanna would say would cost $6.95 in a restaurant, when Will Butler appeared in the general vicinity of the landing in a *small* outboard – winds were already 20+ knots NW and built while he was here. I met him on the shore lugging his heavy tool box in the wrong direction – Helped him carry it up the path. The 3-wheeler needs new timing gears, a job to be done ashore for $100 – and my lawn mower has to go ashore with a bent crankshaft. Returned to my $6.95 breakfast, after seeing Will off in a stronger wind (had dripped coffee for him earlier) when some of the sheep came in line down the road, acting oddly and came in here with a big unshorn male behind them, who proceeded to follow close behind Pauline. The other sheep gathered in huddles in the lower orchard to watch. I yelled at Pauline to keep away from the dirty old man, he'd kill her, and was nearly ready to load the pistol and shoot him – (had lasso in hand but helpless with it) when the truck appeared, loaded down with Perrys, Van and Dwight!

Hail fellow well met! Soo – $6.95 breakfast was left in the stove, I was instructed to leave Mac behind this time – off in the truck to the gather. We missed the wether/ram lamb from here with one hanging low, but *Sweetness* appeared (as well as June and Chaquita). Told Van in the truck (Mrs. Van is *still* away and not telling them when she'll be back or where she is – a month now) if she didn't want him, I'd take him, and he really perked up. "Need someone to keep you warm, do you?" he asked. I said, "Yeah, that too, but I need some help."

Ron and Walter dressed in cotton drill overalls and Ron in the usual green cotton work shirt. Walter finally got out a cap that had ear muffs and pulled them down over his ears. Red, ruddy face. No gloves. Has to "be able to tell by feel." His finger still hasn't healed from the inside. (Margin Note: Annabelle is pushing my pen which doesn't work well in any case.)

From the light I headed off over the barrens and combed the apple fields where the sheep have grazed a labyrinth of clearings. Drove out two small wethers only, but at least came to the hill I was headed for and some sheep which I sent on down to the others.

We left confused wethers and sheep along the way, one in the surf (did he ever muster enough sense to get out of there with the tide rising?) – and I chased a few down from the old house.

I cut strings at the corral and listed the tide-up wethers heaved together on the rocks. Tried to keep the heaps comfortable on eelgrass but didn't always succeed. Van carried more than he should have. Cliff (Hercules/Jason) finally arrived after lobster fishing. We got one big white-face ram and the fellow at my house was a wether (with big ideas) that had missed shearing for *two years.*

Came back to Mac left in the kitchen and the stove *still* going faintly. $6.95 breakfast cold in the warmer.

December 2

Get so far behind in this thing, I put off catching up. Always too bone weary at night to write a sentence. Have decided to tell Nick [Lyons, a New York publisher] I can't write a book until I've lived one. There's no time for writing an island-winter book while one is living through the first one.

Eelgrass banking by the wheelbarrow loads, and some of firewood from lower orchard fill each day. I'm up before dawn, light the kerosene heater, boil a cup of water and then have courage to stir, to start the stove and go out to split wood before breakfast. November 29 then spent on letter to EBW's lawyer and plans for day ashore. Thurs. 30 – in Shelburne, errands and laundry and hurried moment with Joan and back here after dark, low tide, *fog* and near zero (C) – somehow missed the *lobster traps* just off the landing and across the harbour. Nearly missed and lost the mooring as well. Left Christmas ornaments in dark boat by mistake but brought toboggan, along with laundry and groceries in over slippery low-tide poles, saying "God's my help" as I climbed with each load. Hauled punt up on backside, using feet propulsion more than arm-pull, all the way up the skids.

December 3

The gather is over, and a storm is gathering. Eelgrass all around the house now, with need for still more on west walls. SE gale due tonight; W gales tomorrow. My lambs seem all to be present and accounted for. Perrys grizzling that many lambs are missing, but God knows enough were sent off, legs strung up together, away from their mothers into a nearly swamped outboard and thence into Cliff's big boat anchored way up to the corral at high tide. 45 wethers listed for Van. The usual innuendos and outright accusations and counterpoints at the corral. Crofts was "given" one of my lambs this time last year and I confronted Perrys with the fact that "some of my lambs were given away; two I knew about" – (Crofts said Cliff took one that died) – I was then accosted by the fact that "each of us" gave Crofts a lamb in return for stripping his garden – lambs that he nursed through the winter, that wouldn't have lived otherwise. Then Cliff spoke of "target practice" rumoured to have occurred on the North End. I asked him if he had seen the dead sheep/lambs. He said, No, they had just heard of it. (Margin Note: Had altercation with Van over the seal-kill and bounty. He didn't know seals were warm-blooded.)

Perrys asked if I'd have a vehicle here this winter. I said, the 3-wheeler if I could get it to work – they said they were thinking of an automobile/truck-type vehicle – 1984 – then Ron said, "1985, probably." I said, "You've got the wrong person. An ox cart, more likely." I really ought to write Walter a letter this winter. (I wished him well, and asked him to take care of himself; his heart pills were bothering him today, and as we walked together to my upper pasture I told him about Howie, and how/why I was so against drugs.)

(Margin Note: Had time to inspect Hal's cabin. Rice and beans spilled – all his provisions, which I tried to restore to the loft and cover with his various canvasses. No new holes in his roof.)

Mac connected finally with Duchess tonight (Perrys are pissed – but Duchess was working toward it all evening, and Mac slipped his collar. She seems always to be in heat.) – then Crofts evidently didn't want him in the jeep as we came home, so Mac ran behind. I mentioned his age, and craned around to watch him all the way. John kept reassuring me that Mac was "right behind" but once home – I kept him inside while I went to bail the *Molly* before the coming gales – he was sick, threw up when I let him out, and hung off in the bedroom despite talk of "chicken bones, *foods* and vegetabobbles" in his "bowoll" that I have waiting for him since last night.

Turned the kerosene heater on to keep him warm.

The rain and wind are coming now. 10:10 P.M. (Van left me with a pat, saying he'd be back soon.) (Added later: Never did come back.) Lost Mac's leash. In his truck, I think. Told Van about the *other boat,* today with three aboard, that comes picking up the traps Marc [Perry] (apparently) has just put down.

The split log half, put aside for the Franklin on newspaper in the kitchen, looked up at me through its two knots, like a beached, tied wether, long into the night as the storm gathered.

December 5

Decked the house with boughs of cat spruce ... and sang carols as I wove the fragrant branches over the eelgrass. Didn't finish. Big job. Took trees from the south field and path that have been slated to go, but apologized to each as it came down – looked long at the pretty one in the lower orchard, that won't be there tomorrow morning. Gale winds WNW all day – as yesterday! Rained yesterday. Managed to get out to the *Molly* tonight to bail her by light of nearly full moon. Had left the anchor on cuddy, bailing her in the dark last time, after sheep gather, and couldn't get back until tonight to correct the oversight. Am surprised it held there through all the pounding.

Marc tended his traps in a boat much smaller than the *Molly*; then wind increased to around 35 knots. Hope he got back alright. Can't go ashore – Too rough at the landing, and tomorrow another gale is coming, SE, with hard rain. Am nearly out of lamp oil.

Move two loads of wood every evening at sunset and split (before breakfast) what I brought up the day before.

Cold all day.

Yesterday I began the upstairs insulation job and it was hideous. Craning in cramped quarters up over my head with stapler jamming and pink pads plummeting on my head and all around me – having to cut "vapour barrier" by guess gauge in the crawl space under eaves, and tacked them wrong to the beams. Did only one section, but now I know what I've done wrong and will be able to proceed. Must finish boughs first because I think their purpose is to fend off the rain and snow which weighs and washes the eelgrass down below where it should be.

Prizer Regal is keeping the kitchen warm now that it has better than punky to burn, and the help of storm windows, eelgrass, spruce boughs and R20 overhead. Floor is still cold, but I'm not going to insulate the cellar ceiling.

December 7

Gales from WNW. *Molly*'s holding somehow with belly full of rainwater. Temperature is plunging but I can't get out to bail her. Am hoping the tossing sea will keep the hold from freezing solid. -7 to -11(C) forecast for tonight. Snow blowing horizontal to the ground over the south field, and spruce boughs taking off from SW corner of house but holding elsewhere. I've filled five pitchers and the privy basin with rainwater. Will refill all pails and dump the barrel before *it* freezes solid.

Am still in the throes of insulating upstairs under the eaves. Damnable job with the new staple gun jamming every fifth shot and "vapour barrier" festooned in folds around me where I have barely room to crouch and hold a flashlight with my knees aimed at whatever I'm attempting. Somehow finished the west eaves (discovered halfway through it that vapour barrier comes *double* and I was putting double thickness on everywhere). If it holds it will make a *big* difference. A lot of R12 will be left over which I'll probably add to Nathan's skimpy yellow stuff over Howard's ceiling, making it more or less equal to R20. Found "William Perry McNutt Island" in pencil on an irregular board battening a seam in clapboard back under the NE eaves. No date. Don't know whether it was written on a lumber order, or by himself when he built the house. If the latter, you'd think there'd be a date.

Timmy is trying hard to become domesticated. Has been ousted into the stormy night a few too many times for stealing bacon, hamburger and crab meat. Now he makes an agonized effort to stay seated with paw raised while I fix his supper and breakfast. Mac has recovered from his exertions.

Annabelle was stuck upstairs last night and apparently slept on fibreglass pads.

P.M.

Didn't split wood today because of weather and frigging around upstairs with staple gun jamming every fifth staple. Finally had the guts to say NIX. Left all hanging and/or braced under the eaves, figured how much I needed to finish with a stapler that works, and took the leftovers up above the ceiling. Many *bare* places, to say nothing of *thin,* but how Nathan worked himself through the only passageway to the west of the flue, I'll not understand. He must *not* have, which would account for no insulation in the environs W and N of flue. The rest, fairly well laid – but too thin a variety, he must have done as he went along putting up the ceiling. Anyway, I got through, grazing scalp repeatedly on nails overhead – (saw flies matted by the trillions up under peaks and must return, God help me, with Raid) and put R12 wherever, and over the trap door as I slithered back down. Then two pieces distributed over the kitchen where thin spots remained. Storm subsiding, *Molly* holding, darkness descending or I could have gone to split wood.

Since I didn't – since I missed one day, the wood box is now empty at 8:30 as I write. Supper is cooking; water scalding hot to wash my hair in basins and then my filthy self, but I will soon have to turn to the shed apple wood. Have wood ready for splitting, in the shed, but then it will have to dry.

Realize that one's well-being depends on one's brawn. If you can't sling an axe, wedge and sledge, you can't survive here. If you can, all is well, cozy and beautiful. Just don't break a leg, sprain an ankle or develop another tennis elbow.

Health and stamina spell survival.

Also noticed that the filthy clothes I was forced to wear and don each morning to continue the filthy job under the eaves stayed on me quite a while and when I finally hauled them off, down through the thermal underlayer, I saw that my hands were very dirty. WASH HAIR!! TAKE BATH in sink! Put bath mat from shower room in front of sink in recognition of the occasion.

Discovered the purpose of Prizer Regal's upper draft: to cause hot stovetop. (Not so sure, later.)

December 10

Got ashore yesterday, at last, but Sunday, so no mail. Phoned Joanna, but she'd already left for Florida. Phoned Howie twice, but he wasn't home. Talked to roommates in both instances. Phoned Waldo Stoddard [Stoddart] re: 3-wheeler. He says he "might be out this week if at all possible." (weather being the condition). Phoned Brian Race for storm window for living room hall, and b.r. [bedroom] if possible. (Spoke to Rilla).

Visited Mrs. Van, back at last from her reunion. She showed me all her souvenirs – then just as I was leaving told me Van hadn't looked in her direction since she'd come home. Doesn't like her to go away. Refused to eat the birthday cake she baked and left for him. Meanwhile Van tells me she doesn't speak to him ... or tell him when she'll be home. I gestured at something and sent her Godiva chocolates crashing to the floor. Spotless floor, except that I'd just walked in in my boots.

Did laundry, mailed letter to Aunt Ellen (I'd spent most of Saturday afternoon writing in bed with heater on: stress headache from insulation job.) – Then visited George and Susie, George warning me of countless untold winter hazards on island. Susie giggling but agreeing I had to be careful. They worried about me. Dark when I got back, weaving through lobster traps.

Today I laboured in wood and spruce boughs all day long. Rain due tonight. Had salt herring and potatoes from cellar for supper. *Too* salty although I rinsed it three times. Bone weary. Kinked at neck, back and shoulders. To bed early with Minard's Liniment.

December 15

Too much going on to keep writing – SNOW. *So beautiful*; makes me want to cry. Ashore yesterday – coldest crossing yet, met by the Fisheries Dept. in my matted wet hair, waterproofs (Did they think I was robbing traps?) – to see about 3-wheeler which the Cape Islanders took to A & B [Atkinson & Bower machine shop in Shelburne] on Thursday. Needs $175 – some of parts and labour. Ready next Friday. Joge will be here to help. Christmas shopped. Mail delayed. No checks or bank statements that should have been mailed direct on the first.

Thursday, rolled up sheep fence. Van brought me two lobsters and crabs. Trying to keep them alive for Joanna. Took them out to hang off the *Molly* in the snow again today, and couldn't turn the punt back over. Damn thing kept sliding down the skids I'd pulled it up. Even tied, it wouldn't turn. Copper paint all over 2 prs. pants now. Went over boots, icy water, in floating landing.

(Margin Note: -10C) "A cold dome of Arctic air will slide across the Province, bringing snow ..."

Oh, it's so pretty. Split and moved wood as long as I could before breakfast which didn't begin until 2:30 P.M.

Cut final boughs to go around North end and other spots, so the little red house is completely wreathed in evergreen. Then retired upstairs, turning all stoves on, to finish the insulation job. Flies by the trillions again matting the windows and floors. They come from the attic I'm sure now – and have, I hope, now eradicated them.

The insulation job is DONE. Holy Christ – the worst I've ever tackled. (New staple gun from Woodworkers Tuesday. Spent Tuesday night at Joan King's – had to stay too late, to wrap and mail Howie's presents when I found he can't come for Christmas.) So – wintering chores are done – but for two new storm windows, ordered and 2 hours on firewood every day.

Skipper left a plastic bag, (tied tight!), of whelks in the punt for me when I was ashore.

December 17

The whelks have turned purple in the turned-off fridge. The dye for the first royal purple in the Near East, I've read. Gave them a bath. Quickest trip ashore yet, yesterday (Sunday) to do the laundry only – Joanna's patchwork quilt and doilies among other things – and back in three hours. Checked with Skipper and Joan, but no messages. Plan to meet Joanna 12N on Wednesday in Yarmouth. Took pictures yesterday morning in the snow which is now gone, of the little, red, wreathed house with Dad's "Merry Christmas" sign placed in the foreground. Am afraid pictures may be cropped smaller than I expect them to be. Can't figure out the [ ] in the center of Dad's viewing lens.

Stayed in bed late, till nearly 9 A.M. today! – a warmer SW wind. All the snow gone, not cold enough to split wood – but I should have been up and sawing boughs, cleaning house and a myriad of things. All is under a film of dinginess, if not downright filth in the kitchen – (and why I had to wash the patchwork quilt). Stove smoke. Can't let Joanna see it this way.

And the wood burns faster now than I can provide for, it seems. But doesn't heat sufficiently. Baked a loaf for Joanna but the oven wasn't hot enough at the start, so the bread rose and spilled over without baking. Finally cooked on top and not the bottom, so I turned it over and tried baking it more, upside down, in a frying pan while I sawed wood. It only dried out.

Depression could be fatal here. If one just sat down, or stayed late in bed, and didn't get up to do what has to be done. Maybe because the sheep are gone I've felt funky – but probably just the pressure off, with the insulation job done. Still have to clean the mess and dead flies and wash the windows upstairs (Raid) – suppose Howie shows up after all on Wednesday? Actually slept better last night than I have in many. Felt so cozy in bed, with the "warming trend," I guess.

Anyway, once I began sawing boughs I could have continued for hours, but of course it got dark in one hour, as I put the work off until 3:30. Days are too damnably short! Moved all the sawed and gathered wood into the kitchen to dry on the floor (mist blowing all day in the SW wind – while I'd unfortunately left the Franklin wood uncovered) – sort(ed) it, and fed the stove, which suddenly perked up so I had to slow down the fire and finally open up the living room – Too much heat! – in a very short time on dead spruce boughs and twigs. Much more heat from this than the old, dry, punky split trunks. Still, we must *use it all.* Waste not, want not.

Will the whelks live until Wednesday?

The Grand Cayman Islands have just come on Marine Band loud and clear where WQXR should be – 7:20 P.M. – Now here comes WQXR's Dr. Joe Navello ... Bye Bye Grand Cayman ... Nope, the Agricultural Society is meeting at the Georgetown Town Hall. Maybe Joe Navello is in the Grand Caymans.

December 18

All day and night on wood and housecleaning. I wonder if it's possible to get ahead with the firewood, and if it's possible to keep the house clean. A bad case of the dingey-grungeys – from wood smoke. Had to wash everything. Still haven't done living room pictures.

Checked the lobsters – still alive in the box off the *Molly* (so are the crabs) but I've doubts for the whelks in the turned-off fridge. Gave them more water. Maybe a mistake. The *Molly* leaks. Had to bail her again. Starts leaking whenever she pounds into the wind.

The barometer continues to see-saw. Now it's raining. They promised mild Southerlies for tomorrow, but now it's moderate-to-strong North Westerlies. Should be off early enough to miss the worst tomorrow.

December 19 – January 24 – JOANNA'S COMPANY! – no entries.

1985 January 26

Alone again. Deep winter now, powder snow knee deep and drifting three feet or more. A pyramid outside the guest room door, the far walls invisible in the waving drifts across the meadow that seem to climb right up into the trees at the edge of the forest. 5:05 P.M. as I write, and the sun is beaming through the kitchen window, too bright to tell, but somewhere over Crane's Point – still half an hour up. This gives heart. Days noticeably longer, each day lengthening although the snow unceasingly adds at least two inches of powder every day or night and the cold winds blow. Another gale on its way from the Northwest, with -10C to -15C tonight. That's not as cold as it has been.

I've been through the worst of what winter can dole, I *think*, with Joanna, so I'm well indoctrinated for what will follow in the five remaining days of January and four weeks of February. If she hadn't been with me, might I have lost courage? Some of our nightmares, suffered alone, might have been too much.

The *Molly*, an ice cake inside, wedding cake outside, pounding in the gales and freezing spray – worries about the boat are the worst of it. Then worries, laments for the sheep. Haven't seen them or been able to wade through the snow to seek them. Wading to the camp to tend to the *Molly* where we hauled her out of a Westerly gale was enough exertion even for Joanna. We spent *one whole* day, working together, chopping ice off the *Molly*. Lost parts of the motor and Howie's Iranian tool to the bottom of the cove. [This tool is possibly something Francy brought back from Iran, where he lived in the early 1970s.] Maybe I'll find it some extreme low tide. If not, someone else will and throw historians and archaeologists into a tizzy. Alone I might never have gotten the ice off.

Even Joanna, returning after dark the next evening from our delayed "weekly," heaps of bulging plastic bags and oil cans aboard, said as we disentangled from one more threatening lobster trap line in the sub-zero cold, "Mom, I think I'll go home soon." (And over the drifting slush heap at the landing I allowed as how I preferred it in summer.)

She arrived in tears, so desperately glad to set foot on Nova Scotia and be with me again, so sick of the city, but now it was "home" she thought she'd get the hell back so soon. That passed, as all nightmares pass, and once again the supreme beauty of our island enveloped us.

When she arrived the sun had set way down over Roseway. "What's the red light down there?" she asked, alarmed. Now it's sunk behind a low cloud bank directly over the Crane's Point house.

Together we felt the winter clamp down hard. When she came there was still talk of bonfires on the shore – pulling all the dead stuff from the bank while everything had died back and the ground not yet frozen. A job we never got to.

We woke to see our breath in the morning, steaming vapour trails above two heads on the pillow. We saw the potty steaming and the poop hills frozen solid. But Joanna kept remarking that she never felt so uncomfortable in the privy – she "couldn't stand it" – In fact we both often lingered on the wooden seat holes, looking out the door as if in summer. She sunbathed against the house, out of the window, and I even joined her on the tarp one morning for breakfast.

We had "an old-fashioned Christmas" – My fantasy finally realized – Goose in the oven, plum pudding steaming on the stove – tree cut from down the road and trimmed with old ornaments; we sat down to a candlelit dinner after midnight, after cooking all the trimmings all day long.

Tania [Tanya] and Skipper came for dinner one day. Otherwise, and but for a few visits from Crofts and John, and one knock on the door from Waldo, we were alone. The whole time!

New Year's Eve the men from the camp signalled us from their boat, as they returned at 10 P.M., but I'd looked for their light earlier when we came back after dark and decided they weren't on the island. Never noticed their signal. Too bad. We had thought it would be a gas to celebrate with them, but we had our own bonfire (the brush pile in front of the shed) at midnight.

Then the snow began falling sometime in January, and hasn't stopped yet. More forecast for tonight and Tuesday.

Joanna worked like an Amazon on wood, I did some too (what else did I do?) but we never seemed to get ahead – or at least not for long. The necessity, urgency in wood gathering, the dwindling piles – only two left, and I've made major dents in both – and the amount of this punky spruce it takes to keep just the kitchen and bedroom near 68F began to take a toll on my nerves. I'm suppressing the severity of the risk.

What if I run out of wood? What if I get sick, or sprain something, get a tennis elbow again and can't split, saw, haul? I rely too heavily on the kerosene heater. Could easily run out of kerosene, too. Rely too much on the reserve wood supply in the shed. Joanna began dipping too liberally into it. Then she kicked the kerosene heater twice in her stretching exercises and the second time the thing wouldn't light. I hovered over it halfway through the night, changing the batteries, messing around and mumbling in the dark like a crazy lady. I *was* a little crazy. All I'd repressed suddenly came to the fore. We were going to freeze to death –

Yet the heater barely lifts the kitchen thermometer from 40F to 50F in the mornings before I stumble into bathrobe and slippers to start the stove.

Have worn a wool hat to bed many nights: One morning it was 34F in the kitchen. Too close. Put Mac to bed in the top of old ski pyjamas.

But now with the snow it's not so cold. And the days are longer.

Joge was scheduled to leave on the 14th, but we were stuck with a 3-wheeled Honda in the *Molly* and the *Molly* on the frozen stones of Jonathan's former landing. [Jonathan was William Perry's son. He and his father built the house sometime in the late 1850s, and the Perrys lived in it for several decades.] Had attempted to beach the Honda there but couldn't get it out of the boat! – using the gunnels as pivots we damn near busted out the *Molly*'s sides. For two nights we watched over her at high tide, having hauled her all the way up rather than expose her, weighted down, to more Westerlies and freezing spray at the mooring.

On the third day, giving up on rescue from Skipper (who said not to worry if we had to leave it in the boat, that he'd come help us get it out when he tended his traps) – I left "the sign" on the high road and Crofts and Sandy soon came to the rescue. Crofts, to my amazement, hustled down to the shore and heaved the Honda out. Then helped start it, and I drove it up the old roadbed Joanna and I had cleared – and all the way to the house, over the first four inches of snow. Crofts suggested I hook up the wagon and load it with wood while I had the thing running, before we had more snow, which I attempted, but the wood went flying every which way, and Skipper, to the rescue at last, had to push us the final few yards of steep front yard. He came on Crofts' summons and, apologetic, hauled the *Molly* off the frozen shore at high tide with his outboard. Two rescues in one day.

Joanna and I rode double to the light to make radio phone calls explaining her delayed return, tore down the old lightkeeper's road, and back home before dark over frozen plowed ruts. Then the deep snow came, and the machine that has so far cost me $64 (mechanic's trip to island), $155 (repairs and manual) and $3.50 (one screw cap to timing gear) is reposing in the shed, in the way of everything.

Have two more storm windows, one for front "hall" window exposed to Westerlies (I caulked the wall seams in that corner of living room; makes a big difference) and one on hinges for J's bedroom. I ordered another on hinges for study, east. Then will want study north, and other two north windows if Brian will make them for me. 45 bucks apiece for the bigger ones, but he throws in all the hardware.

Rilla was pierced in the throat by a dentist's drill and so didn't fancy an overnight at the island. Joanna and I landed the windows at Jonathan's Point while the Honda sat in the *Molly*. Had to chisel one down to fit. Brian, I hope, will bring the next and plane it to fit (I rigged the hinges, etc.) – as well open the hole in the upstairs flue, a job I still haven't tackled. Nor have I covered the gap in the kitchen flue, spackled, painted and fixed the cupboard. The tin one is now hanging on two screws, telling me I'd better get with it.

I haven't done a lot of things. Still have Christmas notes to write.

Joanna thinks I'll get more done alone. Maybe. But today it was 4 P.M. before I sat down to write what I've put off for more than a month. Stayed in bed reading *Rural Delivery* [a magazine published in Liverpool, Nova Scotia, that Elizabeth subscribed to and enjoyed] and listening to gale reports when I should have been outside splitting wood. Then "flurries" dumped another two inches so I had breakfast instead. Finally out to the wood. Sawed some apple Joanna had left by the shed which I'd hauled from under a snowbank, split wood hauled out from under same, and took the toboggan Santa Claus brought us to the lower orchard, for the second time proving I could, and hauled a load of stove-length logs, straining against the line and calling out "Mush!" to myself at the difficult inclines. Lost only a few pieces a few times. Much easier than I thought it would be through the deep snow, and so once again my courage rises.

Yesterday, alone without Joanna's sensible advice, I found a safe berth (I hope to God) for the *Molly* before the impending NW gale. Had decided earlier I'd run her up the wharf slip (we barely got through the ice, leaving the camp's landing) but saw that the landing is too narrow for the *Molly* and for Crofts' punt to pass it at high tide level. While I was investigating, having left the *Molly* with Mac inside, at the wharf, I looked back to the boat and saw a frantic dog paddle through the ice floes toward the shore. He would never make it, pawing into ice and sliding under. I thought I'd lost him. Ran back through knee-deep snow on the wharf, into the boat, calling him back with all my lungs, and he came, steady and strong to the stern where I dragged him aboard. A person would not have survived. Hefted him up on the wharf and told him to "tear round" which he proceeded to do, ecstatically, shaking himself off and warming up in 50mph careens through the snow. Not bad for 80 years old.

I then had to leave him trembling in the sun while I resurrected an old mooring, examined its shackles and chains, picked a meal of mussels from its tie line, found

Crofts' illicit "crab pot" (full of crabs) tied to a sunken mooring float (no wonder he told me the mooring was "shot down" and I couldn't use it) – basked in the calm before the storm, the -2C sunshine, set the anchor to the second mooring, and Mac and I walked home. Had planned to look for sheep, but the old doggy came first. What a beautiful road in deep snow! Maples and birch stand apart from the spruce – such ancient maples, and birch with bark like burnished pewter – silver birch?

And the night before, returning from our rushed trip to the Yarmouth airport, the first day in weeks of calm water, but readying to freeze all the way across, we had dodged ice floes out of the cove and "window pane ice" all the way across (which had punched a hole in a fibreglass boat from Churchover) alone again and a little scared, praying to the motor to start, "Come on, baby, light my fire" sung in a deathless whisper, then out on the water after sunset but still a pale light over all, new moon and Venus in the Western sky and the island ahead, serene in the snow, deep Canadian snow on every branch and bough, stone and boulder from Horseshoe to corral and the vanishing South end, soft gray and white, gray water, white snow-capped ice floes broken the length of the shore, and from that shore a light in a fish house window calling me home. I snagged another lobster trap, but we didn't stall, and I could pause to see the little red house with the snow-covered hillside framed by forest heavy in snow, and orchards and birch below. How worth the pain and fear; the poling through ice floes in a leaking punt from mooring to shore.

At the landing, dark now and dead low tide, I was cautious over every step and effort. Pitfalls, footfalls, ice, slush and snow. Hauled the badly leaking punt up sitting down, one skid at a time, with legs braced to push with the arms' pull. Told myself it was going to take a while. No need to hurry. Safety first. Had only a few provisions bought at Swim's General Store in Barrington. Left the laundry, undone, in the back of the car (snow knee deep on the C.V. wharf, but a narrow path shovelled when I got back). Mac waited patiently. I loaded the faithful toboggan ("Do you have enough snow to merit this purchase?" I had asked the Robertson's Hardware woman. She was reluctant to say.), extinguished one faithful oil lamp, took flashlight and slowly mounted the path without losing bundles along the way. The kitchen was 48F. Not bad.

And for lunch today I made myself some lobster bisque. Yes, the whelks lasted. We had them in spaghetti.

January 27

Until 3:15 on wood and chores. Keep expecting to have half the day free for desk work, but never do. And I was up before dawn. Although the afternoons are considerably lighter – not dark till after six now – the mornings are dark until 7 A.M.

Mushed the stove oil and kerosene up from the fish house, split yesterday's wood haul and mushed another large toboggan load from rapidly dwindling largest wood pile. Only it and half the far one of very *dry* smaller wood left. Only 4 gals. of kerosene left. -14C last night, strong Westerly today (WNW 30 knots) and cold again tonight. Will fuel and I last?

Toboggan tracks gouge the pristine snow like funrun shoots in various downhill curving directions. Crofts and John (recovered on my vitamin C) arrived and looked around. Plowed my lane again, but no way to get the Honda to it. What a shame I couldn't use it after all the money

I spent, Crofts said, but I said I was better off with the toboggan than struggling to shovel and get the thing started. Now Crofts has the cold so I didn't invite him in. Mean of me, but if I get the thing, I'm in trouble. *Must* work on wood at least two hours every day. Offered to bring him out a cup of coffee, but he declined offer.

The kitchen shelves are dingy again. It doesn't take long. Have started rotating cups so that they'll stay relatively clean. And I'm dingy again. Notice my feet beginning to smell like my brother's socks in the laundry hamper or like "Kearny foot." Will wash hair and take a bath in the sink tonight. It's hard to believe that earlier in January Joanna and I had showers in the shower room. Snow came in during the blizzard and outlined the basin and pitcher with birthday cake frosting. It hasn't melted yet.

To avoid colds meet the vigorous weather head-on with vigorous outdoor exercise, I read recently, rather than huddle by the fire. Well, I'm doing that, and when the weather gets violent, so do I, adding more wood to the load and straining till things pop against the wind, adding wind to the wind, but mine's a lot warmer.

Inside I add layers of clothes to those already on and am getting used to 60F. Anything over 68F is blazing hot. Then the layers peel off, I sweat and bear it. Opening a door would be inexcusably wasteful, considering the violent and vigorous, patient and attentive labour that went into providing that heat. 72F in here now after stoking hard with yesterday's *and* today's splits – and it feels awfully good to be warm. Have door to living room draped and chinked with flannel sheet. Maybe I'm getting sick??

Crofts says he's going in April for sure; they've given him notice, and John has nodded confirmation. [The lighthouse was to be automated, so Bob Croft would be out of a job. "They" was the department of Fisheries and Oceans (DFO).] I'll have to look into the schoolhouse and sheds that will only be torn down or burned when they leave – and write the D.O.T. [Department of Transportation] about purchasing equipment *here* rather than having to follow it a hundred miles to surplus auction.

[This entry included a newspaper clipping from the *Coast Guard* headed: May See Record Snowfalls, January 1985]

January 28

(Margin Note: Annabelle is rubbing against the pen.)

If I were seen en route to privy in the morning, I'd scare people. Gingerly hugging potty and lifting long gown over black rubber boots, old bathrobe dragging under a red and black lumber jacket, I have any old thing on my head so long as it's warm. Evelyn [Elizabeth's cousin in New Jersey] knitted a hat big enough for Ulysses and gave it to me because it matched the sweater she knitted, which has become my winter coat ashore worn under fisherman's waterproofs. Sometimes I grab that if it's handy near the door. It covers me down to the nose. I look through her loose stitching. But more often that hat is left on the bed where it draped my head and face all night.

Worked until 3 on wood again. It's "cold as the hills" and blowing hard.

McNutt's Island Journal 3
January 29, 1985 – March 10, 1985

January 29

Quarter to five and still bright sunlight. Only trouble is I've just finished the routine chores, including several hours on wood, and there's no time left for desk work. At night it's too hard to see to type, and I'm too beat anyway. Haven't yet written those Christmas notes. This old tough spruce is a killer. So is the toboggan haul up through deep snow. But where would I be without these stove-length logs? – Am soon to find out, for the "humongous pile" is rapidly diminishing.

Read late into the night on planting strawberries, and celery, and article on the ale wife, one on sheep – in fact everything in a 1983 issue of *Country Journal* I'd missed. Article in it by Alan Crussow and piece on Devonshire cream by a Gardner who could well be wife of the pair Brian Race wants to bring out here. "Runs a Maritime guest house" – The Tea Cup? – In other words, an astonishingly packed, neglected, issue. There are dozens such from two years back waiting for me to catch up.

Catch up. Can't even get caught up with wood demands ... which would be to stash in a supply for at least two days ahead. Can't get one day ahead (except for the Franklin), and yesterday I was having to hurry out to split wood for the breakfast fire. That's cutting it too close. With seasoned hardwood, or even relatively fresh seasoned spruce, I might be alright. Well, I'm clearing the land and not *wasting* all those wood piles down below.

Bright sunny day, but as usual blowing like hell. Haven't been to the *Molly* since I left her at the wharf. Is she weighed down with ice? Out of sight, out of mind. Have enough to worry about with the sheep. Read last night that Suffolk lambs have low survival rate. Chiquita, Sweetness and June are mixed Suffolk. Along with two others I don't remember seeing at the last gather. Warmer today but still below freezing. Snow isn't melting, but it's shrinking, and now and then an icicle drops and shatters.

February 1

How do the owls know it's February? They've been at it all day: "Whooo'll be mine?" "Whoooo's for me?" More of a lament than a courtship. "Whooooo?" In this weather, I don't wonder.

I spent the morning in bed with yesterday's mail and the *Coast Guard*, kerosene heater, too lazy even to get up and start the stove. Partly because there was practically no wood left. Yesterday's trip ashore was an ordeal I'm too tired to summarize now. January's over. More snow tonight and tomorrow. Joanna's long splits of apple are a godsend – I saw them in half (after hauling them up through the snow) for Prizer Regal, to mix with the punk which is all I seem to be getting now from what's left of the big wood pile.

The lamp oil (33-litre can) and kerosene are still in the *Molly*. Tried again tonight to get them ashore but too risky over broken poles and ice and a tide that doesn't want to come high. More gales coming – but from the east and north. I bailed her again, chopped away the rest of the four-inch thick ice, and hope for the best.

GROUNDHOG DAY – February 2

He didn't see his shadow. First thaw in weeks! Drizzle all day and an ominous stillness before what threatens to be a 50-knot Northerly gale tonight. Bailed the *Molly* twice today, and fell in off the landing both times. Finally manoeuvred both kerosene (20 litres) and lamp oil (33 litres) into fish house. Tides don't get all the way high. If this were summer, three days before the full moon as it is, we'd have extreme high tides. What's a fairly simple operation in summer is suddenly hazardous to limb and life on icy skids and snow-covered plank walks. Can't see where the gaps are, can't set down the cans without having them slip – And the landing is broken now, a critical lapse near the big rock.

I left the two containers in the *Molly* Thursday night, preferring to lose them instead of legs and whatnot, after dark, and had tried yesterday (but this is repetition, I see.) – The whole push is so damned difficult sometimes, one wonders ... (Margin Note: Turning the punt over on icy skids is a suicidal effort too. I left it upright last night but got it turned over today.)

The path is now a slush mire – It had packed down somewhat with the toboggan hoists ... my last load of groceries and laundry (Thurs. night) hauled up in moon glow, overcast sky but a "luster of midday to objects below" except that the snow has been around without melting for two weeks now. "New fallen snow" is coming again tonight when the mercury dips with the Northerly gale.

Toboggan was put to service in Carleton Village, hauling oil cans to boat along with laundry, etc. There I did not yell triumphantly into the night "Excel-sior!" as I did straining the last way up the path to the house. In Carleton Village it didn't yet seem quite possible.

But I've learned never to quit. So tempting, so often, to withdraw with a "some other time." If I'd yielded to the sirens luring me to a warm bed instead, there'd be a cold house, a boat on the rocks, and a few other serious discomforts. (Margin Note: Tried to make chowder on the Franklin. No Go. Had tuna fish sandwich for supper.)

Car didn't start Thursday. Put CAA to early use. Reached Shelburne at 2 P.M. to do two weeks of errands and business. (Left the house at 9 A.M., mushing the toboggan down the island road to the wharf where I found the *Molly* ice-caked, her anchor line snarled around the mooring, and the motor requiring 50 pulls and spark plug cleaning to start. Then Skipper pulled alongside and gave me a haddock and a flounder. He also helped ease the toboggan load into the *Molly,* but the tide was low, the distance long, and the load went flying.

Now I know why the spruce grow up so quickly, sprouting everywhere. The snow is strewn with spruce seed, looking like little brown fly wings.

February 3

Latest "gale" has not amounted to much. Our windbreak of forest to the north muffled it almost entirely, and Jonathan's Point was just enough shelter for the *Molly*. But it's getting colder. Two more inches of snow last night. So much for the Groundhog thaw.

Grace, Maude, Helen, Diana and Sweetness, June and some other lambs appeared at the edge of the north woods. Poor Maude has dark circles under her eyes, but otherwise they looked well enough. I went out to them with apples, both whole and cut up, billing and cooing and calling them my darlings. They just looked at me, and when I tossed the apples they turned away, as if offended. Damned if some crows didn't come down and take off whole apples single-beakedly, ones that were quite a sacrifice, the best left in the cellar. (Put in there green. All the ripe ones rotted. I'll know next time. The green ones are now ripe.) I tried twice with the sheep, but no takers. I think Grace found some later for she was back in the general area. Very puzzling. You'd think they'd be so famished they'd come at a gallop. Maybe they're just plain dumb. Some of them seem half blind. June bumped square into a tree.

I've been telling Mac jokes, and see again what I've known all along – he has a definite sense of humour. I came up from the cellar with three long bony carrots dangling from my cuff and said, "See what the old dark cellar did to Missy's fingers?" He leapt and pranced and pounced in circles, then tore behind the shed and came back wiggling from stem to stern. (Margin Note: He knows the word "fingers" because he gets to "lick my fingers" when there's dog or cat food on them.) Later, he was munching on crab shells from the compost while I was splitting wood. I reminded him that compost would make him sick, but he didn't seem too ruffled. Then I said he'd get "sick as a dog," and he howled with laughter.

A quarter to six and I still haven't lit the lamps. Sun has set well north of the Andersons' house. Last night it was nearly dark (before the storm) when I went down at this time to bail the *Molly*.

Losses lingering today. I must shake loose. This is no place for pain and tears. It is my compensation for all the losses, battles and ordeals of my life and my lot to enjoy it alone. Joanna and Howard are likewise my compensation, both of them major miracles. My blessings are enormous. Why should there still be pain?

For one thing, I think I dislocated a kneecap at the boat landing last night. Still haven't written my Christmas notes.

Annabelle's good form while she waits for dinner to be served is not because she's preparing to bop Timmy, as Joanna suggested. Tonight she sat patiently with paw raised, and Timmy was nowhere in sight. He'd been tossed out into the cold night for having swiped my haddock.

February 5

First time I've ever baked a loaf of bread for myself, but I'm out of bread, so that's as good a reason as any. It came out better than any other I've done on Prizer Regal but I paid for it with dry apple wood from the shed and lumber scraps from the crate in the guest room. Am down to the *bottom* of the humongous wood pile and those logs are firmly frozen into the ground. Deep cold for three days. The coldest nights yet -20C which is -3F. I wear Evelyn's floppy wool cap to bed and by dawn both cats and Mac are pressed against me. Windows frosted, but it was no lower than 42 (degrees) in the kitchen this morning. I put a big piece of dead apple in the firebox before I went to bed, cracked the lids and it burned all the way through, probably for a long while. Didn't start the kerosene heater until daylight.

The snow banking the house helps too and there wasn't much wind. That picked up again during the day, as usual, and the *Molly* is pretty heavy with ice once again. Too hazardous at the landing to risk going out for a little ice removal. Instead I hauled up kerosene and looked for Howie's Iranian tool I lost overboard at a very low tide. Am sure I'll find it when there's a *calm* extreme low. The bottom is rocky there. No weed or mud. I gathered some mussels which I've just consumed, piping fresh, in olive oil, garlic, white wine, parsley and Parmesan. Smack.

All day on wood today because another snow is scheduled for tomorrow. I'm getting weary of my monologues while splitting pesky logs.

Night before last near-full moon lit up the snow like midday on the moon, and it was so cold the path to the privy seemed to send out sparks as it crackled underfoot. I showed them to Mac as we went outside, "Spar—ko's" in the snow and he went half crazy, bounding and pouncing with his paws outstretched trying to catch the elusive diamonds in the snow.

One male and one female grosbeak have been left behind by the flock and at the feeding platter at different times: one yesterday; one today. I hope they find each other. Mankind has no monopoly on greed. These seemingly innocent juncos are as ornery and selfish as any creatures I know.

Now I've heard the stars of *Porgie and Bess* [soprano Grace Bumbry and bass-baritone Simon Estes] about to open at Lincoln Center, on two different artsy talk shows, and they were utterly different people the second time. First, for "Vicky" Gaberough [Vicki Gabereau, host of CBC Radio's *Variety Tonight* from 1980 to 1984 and *Gabereau* from 1985 to 1997] in Toronto, they laughed, joked and poked fun (at) each other throughout the interview. Grace Brumbry (sp?) [Bumbry] also sounded wholeheartedly enchanted with Gershwin's opera and happy about the whole thing. That was CBC. Then last night on WQXR with Bob Sherman [host of *The Listening Room* and *Woody's Children*], the music reviewer who becomes so emotional, particularly over his dead mother, they were downright morose and Grace with a fair touch of animosity in her replies. Now and then they attempted a chuckle by alluding to some of the funny moments I had heard before, he [Estes] rolling his aria r's as Porgie, for one thing, but a tired attempt at humour. She was forcing herself to laugh. How does this happen? Too many talk shows? Or did they not like Sherman? I forget [the baritone's] name.

Good reception tonight, Rampal's flute and other lovely music. Transports me from the hermit's drab duds to gentility, and the beauty man is capable of.

February 6

Now I've started telling Mac stories – about "The Digdee Dogdee who had no foods" – with the winter winds and snows blowing in his doors and windows. He had to go down into the dark cellar to eat hoppy toads and spiders … etc. until Mac comes to the rescue. Only trouble is we end up with two doggies in the little red house, which won't do. So I told him it was just the end of chapter one.

We're in the depths of a *deep* freeze. I spend the entire day keeping stoves going. Had all three working for a while before the wind settled to a moderate northerly. And whacking ice off the *Molly*. Was out there an hour and (a) half. Didn't get all the ice out of the cockpit. Lost an oar but retrieved it. Lucky the wind was on shore – could never have poled against the wind for it or for shore, for that matter. Frostbitten hands as well as feet.

Tomorrow 20-35-knot westerlies, lord help the *Molly*. Don't know whether to move her to the camp skids or leave her at the mooring. A lot easier to do the latter, but I dread the thought of what ice might accumulate, enough to make her drag the mooring maybe.

No chance of getting ashore in this. No Valentines. No mailing the numerous letters I've written. Which discourages me from writing more. Guess I'll read my tax forms. God knows, there are enough of them. Farm losses? Why not.

It's because of the punk I'm burning. Have to feed the stoves with one hand, dust pan in the other. The wood stacked to dry for the Franklin topples over, sending punk fragments and raw earth everywhere. Same in the kitchen if I have pieces stacked to dry. Bless Joanna for her big split apple pieces that I've sawed in half – without that mixed in I'd have frozen long ago.

Crofts hasn't been down for more than a week. Not a boat on the water for several days. It occurs to me that if something did happen, an incapacitating injury or illness, stuck in a window or hole somewhere, I *would* freeze to death, in short order, along with Mac and the cats left in a frozen house. A helicopter has been over ... several loud times yesterday, right over the house. Maybe they reported to those concerned the smoke from the chimneys and me out at the wood pile.

February 7

Foremost and almost only concern is keeping warm. Less than 4 gallons of kerosene left, so must conserve. Cold snap forecast through Monday (Feb. 11) and they don't say it will let up then. Split some old spruce, but it's virtually worthless in this strong west wind -15C (+3F). So I spent some time on dead bay ... remember my clearing project abandoned in September or October? *Now* maybe I'll get those eye offenders in the far meadow. Also brought up more of Joanna's long split apple, *tied* on the toboggan this time which made the haul, if not the tying, a cinch. Even with the apple/bay/spruce combination and door to living room padded with flannel sheet I couldn't bring the kitchen to above 65F. *That* feels positively toasty, however, in several layers of clothes. I've even peeled off the outer upper layer of four. Undressing for bed is quite a procedure with four top layers, three bottom layers, and two-to-three pairs of socks.

Mac heard tonight about the Digdee Dogdee whose beddy walked away.

A watched pot definitely does not boil. (Cream sauce made with cornstarch.) Searching for cookie recipes on packages, the only one I found was for "hermit cookies." Will bake.

February 8

More of same, but colder. "Cold Wave Warning" tells us exposed flesh will freeze outdoors. "Heavy Freezing Spray Warnings" and several additional marine areas listed as partly or mostly ice-covered. Along with these dire forecasts (gale warnings, westerly) which I heard more and more frequently, spending less and less time outside and a great deal at the window watching the gray, pounding waves at the *Molly*'s bow – heaped higher and denser by the hour with ice – a huge ball of ice on the mooring line which I'm afraid bashes the bow, adding injury to insult, with every other wave – watching the "flurries" race horizontally across the meadow, and the ice pile in to the shore, the tidal rocks glaze over like petit fours ... along with these forecasts today come hourly reports for McNab's Island [an island at the mouth of Halifax Harbour] ... perfectly straightforward sort of average (for the day) wind and temp ... – (but not what's here at McNutt's), mentioned after "Shearwater"

– and at the end of the reports comes "Grindstone Island" – which has been either overcast, or mostly cloudy, with the usual wind and low temperature.

The reports come every hour, with different forecasters, who breeze right over "McNab's Island" but seem to stumble a bit dazedly on "Grindstone Island." Now either this is the work of Graham [Ruth VanBuskirk's brother, and Skipper's namesake] or there really is a McNab's Island. I don't know which would be funnier. If it's Graham's doing, I'll have to send him a Valentine. If I ever get ashore. Have list overlapping calendar for Feb. 7th's proposed trip ashore. Errands grow and grow – but some, such as "get and send Valentines," can now be erased. Maybe I'll get there on time to wire flowers.

Chicken roasting in the heat of punky apple chunks hauled up this morning. Last night's apple lasted most of the night, the coldest yet. Didn't have to light heater till dawn. No good splits left. Logs frozen in ground. A few down at the maple tree. Then it's saw boughs. But wind is due to diminish in two days, and temperatures to climb tomorrow. Thank God.

(Handwriting messy because fingers are split, and I've unaccountably begun to hold pen differently.) (Am sipping bourbon, too, but not that much. Maybe in the cold it has a stronger effect.) I clamoured [clambered] through the snow to the tall dead bay in the far meadow, the wind nearly blowing me over and every third step my foot plunging through to above the knee, and found they were not nearly the source of firewood I thought. Much skimpier than they appear from the kitchen window. I brought in some trunks and branches anyway, long since burnt up in the fire box. Maybe deep under the snow the trunks are bigger. However … The firewood situation may be getting critical.

February 9

A miracle. A natural wonder. I am aglow and agog with gratitude and relief. One more day of this and I'd have lost the *Molly*. Possibly lost the sheep, if we haven't already. This morning I saw the ice encroach to the *Molly*'s mooring, then surround her. Ice chunks on her bow were lifting the stern out of the water. The wind picked up from the north, nearly 30 knots, but she was in the lee of Jonathan's Point. This pocket out of the wind left the ice free to form, but the wind kept it, for the moment, from being more than dense waving slush. At the same time the slush held the waves down, protecting her more. I left the toboggan at the lower orchard and went out past Jonathan's cellar hole to see a great arc of ice extend from our shore to close off the cove entirely. At Jonathan's landing the ice was bright green. The *Molly* was caught, bow heavy, in the edge of this arc. If the wind diminished she would be locked.

I managed to draw the toboggan load of quasi-punky wood from across the clearing at the maple tree, and next trip picked up a big apple limb Joanna had abandoned.

Paused to bring in well pails and found the well frozen over, snow inside. The pail broke the ice easily enough ... but one more day of this? The water was down quite a bit. The other wells, full by now, are probably frozen solid at the top. The well-pail rope has been so frozen the past few days that tossing is awkward at best.

Expecting snow, I went to work on the wood splitting before breakfast, and found myself warming up. Had to take off my jacket. Got a lot split fast and came inside to cook breakfast. Went out again to WARM air! The ice chunks had slipped away from the *Molly*'s bow, unnoticed, and she was riding high in the slush. Mac and the cats tore around ecstatically. I said some hallelujahs, and split and sawed the apple limb.

It is *WARM* in the kitchen, on punky wood. 75F with a little apple mixed in.

A "warm front" has come *down* from Labrador warming the northern regions first. (Margin Note: an unusual occurrence …) It will be with us through Tuesday, snow Wednesday, they say, but "warmer than normal." How, then, snow?

Late last night I had Percy Bush on the CB again, endlessly chawing with "Gordon." But this time their talk was all of the weather. From them I learned that Gunning Cove is iced-over solid, boats heaved in the air at their moorings. Same for the north end of the harbour. (Margin Note: "the VanBuskirks," they said.) And the Sandy Point Wharf is more crammed with boats than Percy has ever seen. "Well well well," he kept repeating. "Such a lot of boats I never did see."

He shuddered to think what would happen if there were another storm like the "Ground Hog Storm" they all remember from a Groundhog Day years back. (Probably the one that toppled the privy here, and blew down so many big spruce.)

Apparently the boats are all iced-in together and couldn't get off if they had to. (Margin Note: Where would they go if they had to get out of a storm? he wondered – Said one boat was so covered with ice, all you (could) see were the radar sticking up – "That's a *boat* at the end of the wharf – I thought it was an ice hunk. Well well well.") He also ruminated on the effects of a fire, all locked in together. Among them is a "yacht" – Percy had seen the owners stow half a cord of wood aboard, so he presumed they had a wood stove – Said he heard they were staying in town, "but

I don't know – probably start up the stove to dry her out." Then they spoke of the power of the "pressure" of ice, once it breaks and starts flowing back to the sea. Anything in its way gets taken.

I didn't sleep too well last night. But lookee here! And Hooray! Just as Percy said to reassure Gordon and Ainsley, "Never mind, it'll warm up bye and bye."

Valentine's Day

In the interim I've dashed ashore twice with laundry, errands of two weeks, real estate business, insurance business, estate business, (Valentine mail grams since I never got ashore on time to send cards) back late in mild air (above freezing feels warm) and howling winds, hoisting all over the low tide landing on the toboggan as a sort of conveyor belt. One night I uttered a deep "thank you" to what I took to be Venus, globular in the evening sky, but thought it was too high and southerly for Venus. Later from the privy I saw it was in the west, lower, and, testing later from the side door, I found it gone. Surely too big for a satellite. What the hell was it? And I've just come in from another surprise sighting while viewing (with binoculars) the sheep out on the bar. Looks like a periscope rising tall and straight from the sea. Can't be seen with the naked eye, but there it is with the seas rising and dipping past it. Eerie in the misty light before sunset. I studied it a long while. Got a little scared. If it *was* an enemy sub, it was seeing me.

But then, there's been an odd light out there somewhere on these late returns. Maybe it's a new marker. Will have to investigate.

Not a wood pile left in the lower orchard or clearing. I've moved *all* and spilt most before the thaw took the snow crust. Tied heaps to the toboggan, and all of Joanna's apple splits. Am now burning shed reserve. All else is damp and old punky.

Torrents of rain last night, the sea roaring all day, sopping ground exposed and parts of the meadow walls at last emerging from the snow. Still deep pockets of snow, though, to stumble in over the knees. Bailed a hundred buckets from the *Molly*.

"Gale warnings upgraded to storm warnings," the little man sounded the alarm for all marine areas last night until his little voice broke. The kind of storm I like, *easterly* – the *Molly* in the lee so I can enjoy the sound of the wind at night. Now southerly sending the surf rolling up the harbour and ice sheets and chunks from out of the cove. I bailed the *Molly* at high tide late this afternoon while she rolled on the sea swells that had breached the bar to fold on our shore.

Received Valentine cookies from Mrs. Van "with great adirmation [sic]" after I spent a cozy, exuberant visit with them. Charlie at the Gunning Cove wharf gave me four cod. Made a hideous mess on the stove last night trying to poach and bone them for fish cakes. Will finish up tonight, have stock leftover until it rots in the fridge, and maybe half a dozen fish cakes to take to Charlie.

Mac has learned from watching Bowman to "gather" yellow cats and practiced on Timmy when we got home. Instead of skirting Timmy or balking at the door because of him, Mac had Timmy cornered by the wagon wheel.

So now Mac is telling *me* jokes. Come to think of it, he has before, with his toy doggies.

February 17

I guess maybe I *am* brave. I hope I'm not foolhardy. Whichever, it's tiring ... Returning after dark Friday night in a snow squall ... two inches in the punt and the *Molly* when I got to Carleton Village – was another nightmare, maybe one too many. Still, on all these ghastly ventures I find each time at least one thing to be grateful for. Either high tide or calm or moonlight or warmth. Friday night was calm and the tide quite high. Otherwise black, snowing, and cold. My hair hung in wet matted strings on my face, my gloves were lost in among the cargo so I had on Evelyn's fancy gray suede, took me ten minutes to get them on over wet hands, and they made claws, with the lining all mixed up, where my fingers weren't. Tried taking all ashore in one load, because the boat light was dying and I thought I might not find the *Molly* from the shore, or get back in again. So Mac, 20 litres kerosene, several bags and boxes of groceries, cushions from Stedmans, and stuff from DeMolitor's all wedged in the punt on top of the rollers I had to struggle with in Carleton Village. (Because of high seas, couldn't leave the *Molly* at the wharf.)

We bumped hard against the floating section of the landing, knocking things out of packages and Mac nearly overboard. I inched us over the skids with my foot which went in over boot as the wretched landing sank with my weight. Could get us no farther than the broken section by the big rock. The tide was underneath us. No way for Mac to get ashore, and I had a load to unload.

In the dark I'm not as steady crossing the skids, but somehow I managed to bring the toboggan to the side of the punt, straddling the broken section three times, unloading piece by piece onto the toboggan and dragging the loads up the skids. Finally Mac – who leapt on and off the rock and toboggan until finally he settled down enough to let me pull him a slight distance. Then he tight-pole walked himself to safety. He can see better in the black than I.

I couldn't turn the punt over. Everything loaded on the path, on the toboggan, or stashed in the fish house, but I couldn't turn the poor, battered, goddamn punt over. When the skids are slippery (with ice) it just goes sailing away from me, pulling me down with it after I've heaved it up on its side. I quit. After five or six tries, battered fingers, hips, shins – It's all too damned dangerous. I couldn't see a frigging thing in the snow, with hair in my eyes, and my hands were frozen. Poor Mac, frozen too, waiting so patiently, shivering, blinking his old lashes in the snowflakes – He'll be eleven next month.

Then up the path in the black, with almost extinguished flashlight showing me what had fallen where, but otherwise I lost my way repeatedly.

Once in the kitchen, even the *cold* kitchen as this one was, down to 45F in my absence, I light the lamps, start the stove and heater and am so happy to be home I forget again the ordeal that has brought me here: (unloading the car, hauling cargo by toboggan – or wagon in the snow, as I did this time, out on the wharf, is no summertime outing either. Then the punt rolled into breaking water, a row in the snow to the *Molly* ... where is she?? ... and twenty pulls on the cord to get the motor started ... This is your typical winter crossing I am illustrating) I forget, put away the groceries, dry out the wet things, dangle damp laundry from the lines on the ceiling over the stove, feed the animals and have a bourbon or two. Soon the kitchen warms up, smells of fresh laundry and whatever cooking, and – as I've said – I'm happy to be home.

But what if I didn't get home? What if the motor didn't start on the 20th pull? What if I fell at the landing and broke something? The cats would die, Mac would die, everything in the house would freeze and/or rot – Nobody would know for weeks.

Crofts is away with his only kid. He (Crofts) had the flu before that. I haven't seen him for three weeks or so. John never comes down here alone. No fishermen on the water. Their boats are frozen in. Only that submarine out there somewhere, and they wouldn't help me.

If I had fallen Friday night, I hate to think of the hospitality the sea would have afforded me. Strong winds kicked up massive slabs of ice over the landing that night and broke its backbone. We now have a landing that looks more like a ship's cradle than a boat slip.

Tomorrow strong west winds will probably finish it off. *Every* pole is broken in the center where it was nailed to the big stringer that broke under the weight of the ice. A giant slab is still there, half on the big rock, half angled down on the broken landing. And the *Molly* looks heavy with water, but I can't get to her to bail her out.

Yesterday morning I looked out to see out whole shore jammed with ice, great sheets wedged together and the *Molly* in its midst. She could have had her sides punched. If so, I guess she'd have sunk by now. Can't fathom where the ice came from so fast. I could have run into it returning home. And sunk.

Tired today. Tired yesterday. Then realized, with all these hurried trips ashore (3 this week!) I hadn't been taking my vitamins. Got winded splitting wood this morning. Legs feel cramped. Stiff shoulders, stiff knuckles, strained wrist, hitch in belly and in back.

Among Friday's purchases was a hot water bottle from DeMolitor's. Was so delighted to find one. Couldn't wait to snuggle into bed with it. Boiled a special pan of water for it … the one with pouring flanges – found a hook and chain for it, hung it up and filled it. The drip from the bottom did not stop but formed a continuous thin stream that spilled to the floor. So much for my hot water bottle, whose trade name slogan is "More than a name, it's a promise."

I was brave once. When I carried Dad's ashes home in a paper bag.

February 19

New moon. Heard crows mating today, at least I guess that's what they were up to. One made a hollow rattling sound while it chased behind another that just plain cawed its head off.

I nearly burned the house down. Will have to clean kitchen flue and stovepipe tomorrow if it isn't raining or sleet/snow what-have-you. That unnatural heat, and the smell of house cooking is something I won't forget for a long while. Nor the sight of gray dense smoke erupting from every crevice in the chimney from roof on up. More smoke out of the *sides* of the chimney than out of the top.

Finally have some hot-burning wood (have been sawing boughs again, and standing dead trees) and this is what happens after a long, cold winter of burning damp, punky spruce.

To think that I nearly lost it all … and still might.

February 22

The most appalling mass of gunk came out of the kitchen stovepipe, and the flue was so packed with soot there was barely a hole for draft. The old saw "Waste not, want not" might have backfired in a big way – my determined effort to burn *all,* not to waste the wood piles cut 7 or 8 years ago. Now I know not to burn *damp* punky spruce (and apple, for that matter). Any wood that smolders builds up soot, and Prizer Regal has been smoldering all winter.

Heard chainsaws out on the road, and found two men levelling trees right and left of each confounded electric pole, because the light [Cape Roseway Light] would soon be automated, nobody to look after the lines. One large spruce had fallen over our trail to the upper pasture. I asked if they planned to clean up. "No, we just leave 'em here."

When informed of my trail, though, they obligingly said they would "chunk up" the tree for my stove. Said I could burn it now. Much better than what I've been burning, they said, when they came to the house after learning of the chimney fire.

They helped with the ugly task I was in the midst of, one of them climbing the roof to push the brush through the kitchen flue. As he had required the stepladder up the roof incline, I clamoured [clambered] up to do the Franklin flue, but he followed me anyway. That one was okay, although painted black inside, but the pipe was no lily. *All day* Wednesday on pipes and flues and firewood. Thus once again no letters written to take ashore Thursday.

"Sap starts running the full moon in March," they told me. I could burn the spruce right away. Friday I brought down a toboggan load and split it like a dream. One swing of the axe, and large "chunks" fell apart. Split a whole toboggan load in jig time and brought it in before the oncoming southerly rainstorm.

Well, they were wrong. Put two splits on a hot fire and returned later to find the stove cold and smoldering. Worse than wet punky! I had noticed sap when I split the wood – it ruined my going-to-town dyed corduroys – and once inside the house the wood felt wet. What sap is there is right under the bark, though, and I found I could dry the wood fairly fast over the stove.

So, I conclude the groundhog did have the right idea after all, when he stayed out of his hole this year. Labrador's warm air that melted our deep freeze must have gotten the sap stirring early. More warm air today, after strong southerlies and *rain*. What's more, the full moon in March is less than two weeks away. I should have followed my own common sense before chucking the wood into the stove.

Now I'm afraid I'll be too late to prune the apples. Or to get maple syrup. Still haven't phoned for the syrup bucket sets.

I get nothing done on time. It's a constant push for firewood, bailing the boat or chipping off ice, tending stoves and lamps and attempting to keep some order. While trips ashore consume whole days and put me behind again with the wood.

I want to keep splitting the spruce while it's so easy, but I can't burn it now and need wood to burn. Everything's wet today. Will have to saw down a dead tree for today's provision. And *bail* the boat. Letters to write, taxes to do, sewing machine yet uncleaned and fixed, kitchen chimney still gawking at me – jobs that were to be completed before March – The unfinished makes me toss at night. Even have dreams of wasting vast amounts of TIME. And am.

Couple of dozen sheep at the very end of the bar through yesterday's strong winds and rain. Some of those gusts must have been over 50mph.

After cleaning the hideous flues and pipes, filling three coal scuttles with soot and creosote flakes, I listened to the wind in Prizer Regal's flue as the clean draft took up a clean, hot dry fire of dead apple and dry spruce – poured myself a drink, lifted it and said, "Cheers, God."

February ~~24~~ 25

The signs are here! Tiny red buds on the apple in front, the one I had planned a serious pruning for. The first lobster boat of the "spring season" headed past the house for the open sea this morning, so unfamiliar a sound of Chevrolet diesel (or maybe this one was Mercedes) that I stepped outside to wave to it. The ice has retreated from harbours and coves, and the boats are free again. Third day in a row of above freezing. Yesterday was balmy. Today mist and fog. May have to start the fridge, if another day of this. Went gathering ice at the "crock hole" I cleaned out last fall off the fish house path, put beer in the rain barrel, which still has a solid block center, and cleaned out the outdoor cooler. The ice packs in the bottom were *still* frozen, the chicken I pulled out last night still slightly frozen inside.

My four lamb yearlings have been here several days, nibbling at nothing in the sopping ground. [Island sheep live on kelp, a kind of seaweed, washed up on the shores in the winter.] Still snowbanks in the far meadow, on the wall, and in frost pockets everywhere, but most of the ground is exposed. Can see the buds coming, stems and stalks taking on the colour of rising juices. Birds have begun to sing, and maybe my lambs can read the signs too.

Rolled out the Honda yesterday. The damn thing has been in my way for two months, thinking for sure I could start it in the warm sunshine. No dice. I hate the thing. Wanted to ride to the light and find out about the Crofts' boy, but along came Crofts himself ... first visit in a month ... gave the cord one pull with the choke off, and it started. So later I rode to the north end before sunset, assessed the tree-felling havoc wreaked by the Department of Transportation along the roadside, saw some birch and maple for next winter's wood, went on with the Honda into Louie's field, past the house and nearly to the horseshoe before I had to stop and walk because of deep snow. Saw very few signs of my sheep and began to worry till I found a bunch of them, northerners and some of mine, out on the horseshoe. Helen looked *quite* pregnant. I'm afraid it's from Maude's wether (or not?) and if so, due soon. May it continue to be springlike! Think I saw June galloping the other side of the beach bank and Wanda under a ton of fleece. Those two, and Maude, have been my main anxieties. Have not seen Maude since the dark circles under her eyes.

A little more time for living now that it's getting warmer. God, how I welcome it! Might even get caught up with paperwork (never!) if I don't have to be tending two fires constantly. And if can stop looking out the windows.

Don't know how I did it, but I've gained a day. This is Sunday, not Monday – therefore the 24th, not the 25th. Couldn't understand why today's weather forecasts were referring to "Monday" as though it were not the present. *Well,* that eases off some of the time wasted!

These are all sugar maples here, Crofts says (he came tooting in again like Flintstone's friend on his little 3-wheeler) but I'll have to make sure before I start drilling holes and hanging buckets.

The funny, fat black and white water bird Mac and I have spotted lately off shore must be the "Common Murre" or "thick-billed Murre" but this uncommon water bird swam in a squat with neck extended downward, not like any pictures in the bird book (field guide). A "Common Eider"? No yellow bill that I recall.

February 25

Unscheduled gale from west (to) NW. The *Molly* like a bucking bronco, ten-foot waves in close succession. Wrote a good (it seemed), irate letter to the Department of Transportation about the cyclone-effect along the road, and their tendency to burn up valuable stuff or leave it to the vandals, all before 9 A.M., and congratulated myself. Then spent the entire day looking for the name and address of the man in charge. Never found it. Must have thrown it out. (Burned it.) Soot and grime all over everything. Thought I might write a book called *Hermit Soot*. Then decided *Hermit Hash* would be more appropriate for Nick's list, although I'm sure he'd prefer *The Lower Orchard*.

It's getting colder. Again. But I know now that spring isn't far behind. I've seen the signs, smelt and felt them.

February 26

"*I'll* build you a wharf, Mrs. Hyde," said John.

February 27

Spent a good part of last night and today daydreaming about all that John could do here if he stayed a while during his unemployment. Major accomplishment: got the flipping Honda running all by self. Brought a cartload of eelgrass to the new garden section from the Indian Point beach and then a load of "chunked up" spruce from where the men left it on the trail to the upper pasture. *Westerly* gales coming (*NW* they tell me), along with plunging temperatures and freezing spray. Nothing to do for the *Molly* now but pray.

February 28

She held okay. Cold. Spent an *hour* splitting *one* log for the Franklin – then sawed and split apple, tried some more of the new spruce but found it pesky (maybe fatigue?), brought down the dead tops of *three* trees that the "Groundhog Storm" had pushed over. Have nearly cleared up the spot to the right of the path to the lower orchard, a mess-place I'd thought there was no hope for.

My four lambs (yearlings) still here, lying down against each other in the sunshine. Such stoic darlings. If I tried again to feed them, they wouldn't understand.

Blue jays got their seed again after acting like starving beggars.

Mac has been a-courting three times today, returning with ice on his beard and belly and singing me songs. When I kept working at the treetops he took a case of the shivering fits, so I had to pile him up in bed by the stove. 18 miles running to court today. Not bad for a 77-year-old.

Timmy has a plugged ureter, poor S.O.B. Not as bad as Norman's. I give him vitamin C, w/the homoeopathic remedy made from stinging nettles, and the acidifying chemical gel the vet gave me. Wish I had all this for Norman. Re-grieved for him a full five minutes … PAIN …

Precise, rosy sunset well north of Crane's Point. I have a swing now, up in the trees I've cleared and topped. Straddle a leaning dead trunk high in the air, bounce up and down and watch the sunset!

Two dead trunks leaning side by side would make quite a lot of firewood, but as long as I'm not desperate, I'll keep the swing.

MARCH (!) 2

In its usual fashion March has blustered in upon us, keeping me grounded to the island while letters I wrote a week or more ago gather hermit soot on the shelves and table. Mine to Well's College Alumna's new computerized info center gives my employment as "recluse" and is besmottled with ashes, soot, cat paw tracks and doubtless some pan drippings.

The house is dingy as all hell. Everything in kitchen needs to be washed AGAIN – wood smoke and soot particles on every surface, dish, quilt, etc.

Came back from a long walk to fire laid in Franklin, which I touched off and in five minutes had kettle boiling for tea and the house warming up. (P.R. had burnt out.) Opened the Franklin's doors to a handsome fire of apple and better-quality spruce log, sat down to enjoy it, called the animals in, and wonder(ed) soon why the air was looking dense. Stood up and my eyes watered. *No reason* I can see for a smoking fire this time, SW wind, hot fire, but the house was filling up. Had to open the front door, shed door, study windows and give up all the heat. Damn. What a disappointment.

But the warmth is back now, doors closed. Will have to investigate chimney again. See if I pushed the pipe in too far.

Yesterday I got to like the Honda better. Started it without too much effort and ran it, off and on, most of the day. Took stepladder to the Rennehan house and got all the shingles I could reach with it. Brought that back in the cart. Then tried to haul the long section of new chimney flue but it wouldn't budge. Either frozen in or dug in or I'm pulling from the wrong angle. Left the long rope there and will try again.

Took the Honda and cart into the upper pasture where I'll get the fence posts and poles (to help clear within the walls) and lopped boughs off from the logs the road crew left and brought back all I could, clearing the entrance to the upper pasture in the process. Will have to get at the maple and birch along the road if my letter to the Department of Transportation doesn't take effect. Of course it's still here, unmailed, with the rest. *Must* read the chainsaw books and get going. Another task I keep putting off. Can't be that dangerous to saw trunks that are lying down.

Had planned to take the Honda to the north end, look for my sheep and pick up a cartload of eelgrass on the way back, then go down to the corral, fix the fence post holes and get some *clams* at low tide, more eelgrass if easily accessible and look for sheep from the old clearing to the shore and back. Then go to the light tomorrow for gutters, sawbuck, coal and look for sheep there.

All those plans went awry when I left my post at the dead tree in front I had planned to bring down. Had in mind looking for my four yearling yews [ewes] because a big black dog had been running in their direction. Followed the shore to Indian Point, then out on the point and around the head of the point's cove (first time ever) where I crossed two small brooks, found a mast with halliard [halyard], shackles, and thimbles all intact (must return with help), several useful items, an intricately painted buoy which now hangs over the kitchen stove, and discovered sheep haunts I hadn't known about. One of them brought me onto an odd hummock which tapped hollow under my shepherd's crook. May be only frost heave, but I'm certainly going back with shovel.

Found a once-lovely cast-iron stove dumped off the road and its grate completely intact. Might fit Master Climax, though too short, I think. Followed the shore all the way to the north end where I discovered a stone wall I hadn't met before but readily saw that the sheep knew it well. A dead ram lay there with a "Blue Island" tag, #216 – one of Anne's swapped with Cliff, I imagine.

And there were all my dear friends in clearing: Maude still alive, Wanda with her June I was afraid hadn't survived, Diana, Grace looking very pregnant (if she's due soon, the sire has to be Maude's son "Wether-or-Not") and Helen looking pregnant too. Kay was tall and stately, but what a lot of weight she's lost! I think Pauline was among them – another white face. They all look quite different than in summer. No sign of the usual north-end tribe. *So elusive* they are, except for three wethers missed last summer. Two of them took tumbles while I watched, rolled right over and righted themselves, but one of them had wallowed in a tidal pool before he got up.

When I got back to the house my dear girls were right here in the meadow. Tried to bring down the tree and gave up. Decided it was ridiculous, with bow saw binding, when a chainsaw could take care of it in a minute!

Read in *Country Journal* (year old) "Par for the Cord" – A fellow brings down, saws up, and *splits* and loads his pickup truck with a cord in one and (a) half hours – I guess he doesn't talk to himself and make wry, facetious replies to his comments to slow him down.

Torrents of rain, now. The *Molly* unbailed. Plunging temps due tonight and 25-35-knot NW'ers tomorrow. Will have to get out and bail her in *this* before dark.

March 5

The days go by with gale after gale, last night's easterly bringing six inches of snow, then sleet then warm air with SW winds and rain. The *Molly*'s ice dropped off but she wallowed in rainwater, melted ice and snow and general leakage. I got out to her tonight on good high tide that let me avoid the floating, broken-up landing altogether. Strong NW tonight with -6C expected and strong northerlies tomorrow, so still no trip ashore. Now I hear there may be a mail strike March 16. I've *got* to get the taxes done and mailed before then, but haven't received all the statements.

Am running out of stuff. Mac finished his last can tonight, and last dry food. (8kg. bag left in the car!) Timmy is plugged up again, receiving homoeopathic medicine and vitamin C., Goff's Low-ash food, salt and no dry food now.

Baked bread yesterday, made mayonnaise today. Mustering up casseroles with noodles and cans. Have herring, potatoes and carrots in the cellar but no more lemon.

Have developed case of the klutziness, dropping everything I pick up (broke a nice old spice jar) and bumping into everything near or adjacent to my trajectory. Knocked over and split the antique mending holder so had to take time out to glue and bind it. (Later Margin Note: tumour already??)

Two weeks since chimney cleaning, so I opened Prizer Regal's pipes and found plenty of soot inside. So much for "Safe-T-Flue" I've been religiously sprinkling in according to instructions. The Franklin is tormenting me. Smokes like all fury every time I open the door. Why oh why? Must find out. It's heating the whole house to +70F while NW blows -3C (Two different thermometers going here.) Also cooked my supper. Becoming a Marion Gray house around here. [A lace maker and expert in lace with the Metropolitan Museum of Art, Marian Powys Grey (1882-1972) lived in a dilapidated house in Snedens Landing, "held up by a spell," in the words of Mary Ann Miles in a *New York Magazine* article, March 12, 1990. Powys Grey published *Lace and Lacemaking* in 1953, a key work in the craft.]

Pruned all the dead limbs from the big old scrappy spruce at the edge of the front yard. Had thought of bringing it down altogether, but it's a fine climbing tree, and looks infinitely better now. Don't know what I did all day yesterday other than split wood. Well below zero C all day, blowing like hell. So what else is new? Can't seem to get those letters written or my taxes started. Puttered with the spices today for a few hours.

Dreamt I was teaching again, a class I had to contain in an L-shaped room, and stroll from one section to the other with my unprepared lesson. When I'd leave one section the kids would just go away. And I never remembered to take attendance so I couldn't know which ones were cutting, which were absent, which had just walked out. I threatened them with "ditto" questions they'd be graded on – questions on the "lecture" – but I knew I'd never get around to writing them up, or, if I did, to grading them, and there was nothing to write questions on anyway, since nothing had been taught.

Crofts and John dropped off some birch from the wire-clearing. Crofts does all the talking. John nods. Now they're staying through June, so no wharf/landing until July, if then.

In attempting to ask if John had any time off while at the light I mentioned that Van and Barry Crowell took turns at shifts and had time off otherwise ... That I'd never see both of them away from the light at the same time. (Crofts had already said the job was seven days a week.) With this he became very defensive. He had come down to check the boat, which was part of his duty, after "looking around" to see that everything was all right. Meanwhile, his wife was on duty – or on call, I guess. They "never leave the light without an adult there." But John hedged about coming down here. "The helicopter might come in just then," he said. "You never know."

Forgot to mention I ironed all the fancies this morning without smudging once. Kept three irons going, after cleaning each one in kerosene first, and ran them over wax paper before the first swipe from the stove. How many irons do you have on the fire? Ironing ... to iron ... an early instance of verb drawn from noun. The irons here are true "irons." Fancy.

March 6

Well below freezing all day (-8C) so I split all the spruce from the road crew's "chunking" and the birch that Crofts brought down. Warm weather coming this weekend. Felt better about the diversion from other pressing matters when I realized I was rebuilding the shed's dry wood supply

… to go in this summer … so I am freer to deplete the old apple that's there.

Climbed up on the roof before breakfast in a NW rising gale to look down chimneys. Took apart the Franklin pipe and other than a new build-up of soot despite the "Safe-T-Flue," all I could see was that the two dampers weren't quite in line. I straightened them, and the pipe, leaning it a little bit backward, and Presto! She draws!! Am writing this by an open fire at 10 P.M. Haven't had Prizer Regal on since breakfast (low on stove wood). Took a bath and washed my hair with kerosene heater nearby. Ashore tomorrow: – "*Light winds.*" First time in two weeks. Mac had to eat cat food tonight.

Three yearlings are back but no sign of Chiquita. Mac was gone nearly all day. Returned crying for his missed breakfast, and covered with ice. Timmy's plug has cleared – patience and homoeopathic remedy, vitamin C and salted food. If only I'd known this with Norman, rather than panic each time and drive 250 miles to anaesthesia and catheters. Thank God I don't have to think "If only …" with Howie's illness. Maybe the Norman experience contributed to Howard's cure. No more panicking and rushing to hospitals. Trust in nutrition.

Trust that Chiquita is back with Kay (Che).

March 10

A gentle misty evening, pink and powder blue. While I pruned an apple tree in the north field, a flock of homeward Canada geese honked and pumped their wavering V high overhead. I waved to them, said "Welcome home."

I dare to think I've made it through the winter. Even sauntered to the privy this evening without thinking to put on a coat.

Mac, meanwhile, has fallen in love, forgotten his allegiance to Missy and stayed away a whole night and a day, so yesterday I had to chase after him afraid the horse might have scared him off a cliff at the light. Took the 3-wheeler and cart to pick up wooden gutters tossed over the cliff ("discarded"), to route out the sawbuck I had seen in (continued Book 4)

McNutt's Island Journal 4
March 10, 1985 – April 30, 1985

March 10, 1985

(continued from Book 3) the woods near the bunkers, and to shovel some boxes of coal. Also took binoculars and shepherd's crook. Found Mac blinking and whining but he couldn't stay with me. Had spent all night on the Crofts' porch. Went on a sheep walk (without Mac) – lovely to be down on the South Shore again in a mild breeze – warm enough to have my beret off for a while. Even got a sunburn.

Made some grim discoveries. One of my three-year-olds dead and torn asunder, and a beautiful healthy-looking blackface ewe of Van's, dead only a day, if that, as though she had dropped in her tracks, on her knees beside a well-worn sheep trail. A rock rose beside her and one hind leg might have been broken. The crows had already taken an eye and some bites here and there. Blood was fresh on the ground under her face. She seemed at first to have been gored by two horns in the hindquarters but I guess the holes were made by crows. From a hole in her belly a yellowish wet, fleecy length dangled – could only have been a lamb's tail. What else? I prodded a bit with my knife but could see no more of the lamb, and the exploration was almost more than I could endure. She was lovely still, in this condition, and I called her sweetheart and poor darling.

Walked on past Sloop Rock without finding more but did not get under the trees nor up in their grazed high ground.

The Honda I'm calling "Babe." [Babe was Elizabeth's family nickname.] She starts for me now. Doesn't like to be choked ... It's amazing.

Thursday I got ashore for the first time in two weeks. Spent nearly two hours in the P.O. dealing with my mail that required dealing with. Frantic rushing all day (after delays: half an hour to start the boat; half hour to unlock the tailgate. Gail V.B. [VanBuskirk] came along and turned the key for me). Left a packed suitcase in the laundromat, remembered as I headed for C. [Carleton] Village after dark, went back and the bag was still there. Incredibly lucky.

Luck continued. Blood-red full moon, light wind beginning to build – the motor gunked a spark plug and I sputtered across to the wharf where I unloaded all but a wheelbarrow's worth for the landing. 43 litres of stove oil up with the hoist that wouldn't swing over. So I swung on the rope like Tarzan till I got the keg on the wharf. New garden tools, laundry, 8 kilos dry dog food, crates and boxes of groceries for Chris Hemeon who was supposed to arrive today to work a week with the chainsaw but who didn't show – maul sharpened with new handle, everything tucked in a corner by lobster traps and covered as well as I could in the dark with plastic and snowmobile suit Mrs. Van had given me that had gotten stove oil tipped all over it and been dumped in a laundromat machine (that's when I forgot the bag with laundry – had already put the basket in the car) and was still wet. I put a shovel on top of the big box of new tools and left in the dark for our landing.

Wind up more, clouds over the moon – Mac was waiting for me, whimpering and crying. He had been left because he had taken off for the light just before I had to go ashore. Soon after we got to the house the winds began to roar, later it snowed in its usual horizontal before the gale and by morning it was changing to rain. Dreading the whole ordeal, I went out to the shed for the Honda; it started on the first pull!

I hooked up the cart, put the big tarp and rope inside and steamed off through deep puddles, ice and snow for the wharf. There I found everything as I left it, nothing blown away, nothing even wet except a bit of flour at the top inside the Coop's plastic bag. Nothing got wet going home straight to the back door, all folded securely inside the tarp and tied. At last things are working well! The way they should be.

But still no Chiquita with my other three yearlings, and no Chris Hemeon to bring down the trees. What with going ashore, a day of rain, a day at the light, and expecting Chris, I've been using the dry reserve wood and am now running seriously low. Must prune apples, currents, gooseberries ...will my tax return ever be filed? – And fill the wood boxes again.

And again I owe so many letters.

March 13 – Day after a SE storm

Went down to bail the *Molly* and found all ice and snow gone from the path for the first time. Still some lingering patches in the far field.

Chris never showed up, but Russell Hemeon came with a pail full of small lobster for me. Food is in overabundance here, turkey legs and chicken defrosted, cooked picnic ham and pot of chili uneaten, vegetables going to waste, bread, donuts and pie going stale, and now the critter box crammed off the *Molly*. May they not suffocate.

My little Japanese pruning saw works magically. Have filled the wood boxes and cardboard cartons with dead apple, and hot fast fires in Franklin and Prizer Regal may be burning off some of the tar coating the flues. Too hot in the house. Went without long johns today for the first time. My corduroys flapped in the breeze.

Ground is sopping wet, just right for pulling spruce seedlings if I ever finish the letter to Joanna. Will I ever start my taxes?

March 16

A retake on winter, and the luck of the Irish with me – (St. Patty's Day parade today in New York, and tomorrow Barbara will be planting peas.) [Barbara Moment of South Nyack, New York, was a friend of Elizabeth's. She and her husband Jack, both artists, visited McNutt's in the early 1970s.]

Went ashore Thursday (14th) to find that Floyd Hemeon decided it was taking a risk to send his son out here. (Floyd's idea in the first place.) Got G. & S.'s [George and Susie's] ice cream maker but no time to deliver it. 2 kegs of kerosene. *Mail.* Came back an hour past high tide in a building Westerly with gales forecast. My landing too rough so I ran up hard on the camp's skids and tied fast. The punt was inside the *Molly*. Went back next morning for the kerosene and found her okay but leaking as the tide came to her transom. Planned to caulk at low tide – filled the Honda cart with eelgrass while I watched the tide come in.

At high tide (after riding back with eelgrass to garden) the sea washed clear over the transom and swamped the stern, dunking the motor as deep as the stop button. Nothing to do but watch. Went back at sunset, Babe the Honda starting for me (with effort) bless her, and I used the headlight for the first time. Managed to open padlock and lift motor off transom. (Let plug out, drained *Molly* first.) Put it high in the punt on stern seat. Did not caulk. All too wet. Thought I would today at low tide.

Meanwhile, in the wind blast at house I pulled some spruce in the East field and got sidetracked repeatedly by brush along the fish house path (thought I had cleared it all, but with the ferns and grasses died back I find more) ... and by other diversions. Eelgrass loads in the Honda cart, etc.

This morning I returned to check on the *Molly*. There she was, the wharf still standing (gale NWer's in the night) and I thought all was well until I saw as I approached the landing, the punt with the motor *out of* the *Molly* and swung clear around facing the water. I expected to find the whole stern of the *Molly* smashed out, but there she was, intact, full of water on the skids, her after-seat hurled forward (punt had been resting on it) and floorboard that held brace for the seat missing.

None of this could I believe. The motor didn't even seem wet. The punt had not been tied, but there she was, facing out to sea, her oars and little bailing scoop still in her, a crust of frost inside. Later I found her painter snarled around the *Molly*'s anchor in the cockpit. This had held her on the skids. One enormous wave must have tossed her out of the *Molly*. The gas can was upside down under the middle seat. The fuel line is frozen (no. Just doesn't squirt unless punched.) so I don't know if the almost-full gas tank has seawater in it or not. Will take a sample when I can.

... *So.* I went on to Amos's for eelgrass, (having knocked the plug out) and home for lunch – then back again to plug *Molly,* caulk transom and *haul* punt with motor high on the skids. Got more eelgrass.

An infernal blast of westerly gale made working outside unpleasant but I split some spruce felled last August by Francy and Howie, and gathered what I could without getting involved in pruning again.

The front flower beds are poking up crocus, daffodils and tulips! No fence yet! And below freezing all day. I added heaps of eelgrass to the wood chip mulch – (for warmth tonight and to discourage the sheep) – Back to the *Molly* again. (Honda taking me each time, after exhausting struggle with pull cord.) Only a little water in her stern, from breaking waves. Tide doesn't go very high in the day (3rd quarter moon) but seems to go higher at night. Or the waves do! Wind had begun to shift back to Westerly from NW which gave the boat some lee but a few waves splashed in even so – with no weight in the stern. I stayed until I was sure the tide was going out again. Tonight it's supposed to diminish from the West, then shift to South and SE – but next we have snow and NW gales again on Monday!

But the bulbs are up, and the sun set over the apple trees at 6:30. It was still light enough to see well at 7:00 P.M.

Fire going hard in Prizer Regal all day but never got the kitchen above 65F in this wind. (Good wood, too, but never fully stacked.)

Am giving Mac halibut oil, capsules, kelp, bee pollen, and brewer's yeast. He's been looking scrawny since his marathon at the light.

Timmy and I gawked out the window together at the sink, as we do from the bedroom window. I don't know if he sees what I see, but we both stay entranced and/or alert for the same amount of time.

None of the animals likes the wind. I wonder how the sheep can stand it.

March 17

Dawned blue, golden and calm, as though nothing out of the ordinary had happened. Daylight at 6:15. Snow coming. 15cms! And *more* wind. Tomorrow another NW gale following the snow. May the *Molly* hold out. Must *prune* ... *and* get a load of wood. Reserve is very low.

How easily I become sidetracked! The storm held off until nightfall, *fortunately* as I had meandered off from the gooseberry pruning below the front bank to clear dead bay et al. and heap it up on the bank. Spent nearly the whole day at this, though I did "prune" currants and gooseberries, worked on the front apple which I've decided to let remain a two-trunked apple for the sheep (they've exposed roots from both trunks which I'll have to cover somehow) and prune the hopeless cherry some and the two apples by it. There is far more here in the pruning dept. that [sic] I can ever manage alone during "early Spring."

Sped off in the Honda to check the *Molly*. She was fine on calm water – tide higher than before. It seems that on and around the quarter moons the tide doesn't go very high (3rd quarter). Maybe on the 1st quarter it doesn't go very low. Will have to look into this.

I'm *glad* the kid never came! I've saved $200 I can pay Howie, haven't been imposed upon, can take more time deciding what falls and what doesn't (he would have cut the front apple tree in half first off), and the food has kept! Just took a perfectly fine chicken out of the outdoor cooler. (Bought it frozen ten days ago). And how could we have gotten through these storms together? I'd have to get him off tonight. Then where would I put the *Molly* for tomorrow's gale? (Maybe the motor won't start ... Then he'd be here for *quite* a while.) Uh-oh ... found chili in the warming oven, scalding hot. (These fires of small dead bay, etc. are very hot.) Had some, even though I'm rapidly baking a chicken, steaming rice and finishing off the spinach and broccoli lest it spoil.

Even with snowstorm coming, I find my long johns too warm for the house. Maybe it's the hot fires ... door to living room open ... or maybe it's *Spring* coming!

March 18

Could not rescue the Coast Guard today with *Molly* and motor separated, high up on the skids. Crofts came in looking wild, snow bespattered, and begging a favour. Could I take him ashore? His boat had *sunk* – Broke from the mooring in the gale that sent the punt flying out of the *Molly*, dashed on the rocks and sank when towed off. He says he hasn't bought groceries for three weeks. I offered ham, potatoes, eggs and milk. He left with a bag of donuts.

Snow now, northeasterlies – Tides going very high with the new moon three days off. Northwesterlies tomorrow. Say another prayer for the *Molly*.

I am staying INSIDE today writing letters, squaring desk work ... ordering seeds, I *hope*. Maybe I'll be ready soon to start my taxes.

March 19

Helicopter back and forth and circling today (to ferry the Crofts) so for the time being I'm not needed. Wrote letters all day, long ones. I think I'm beginning to feel the old necessity back in the writing hand.

March 20

First day of Spring?? Gales, gales, shifting all the hell around. The *Molly* still at (on) the camp landing. Winds from SW in early morning and building all day to 30 knots. Went down not early enough and put big car tire between her side and dock. Stayed to adjust as the tide lowered. Haven't been back since, but should have. Pruned apple trees instead. Walked home through the woods. Found the small, ancient open well again. No sign of Grace and her lamb-to-be. Kay and Chiquita rejoined the two yearlings here. (Diana's lamb is gone, probably joined up – I hope – with Mama when the older ewes came through.)

Am having chicken hash cooked on dead apple twigs – one very like unto the other. "Waste not, want not" made me nearly lose the whole chicken noodle (kit and caboodle) (chimney fire).

I love being in trees again, even in the wind. Vowed when I was a tomboy that I would never stop climbing trees. But the years intervened, and when I tried again, after raising two kids, it wasn't easy. Not the old limber strength in arms and legs. But it's back now. Or something approximating the old agility and surefootedness. And this little Japanese pruning saw works so well! Zap! – as I wrote to Howie.

March 23

Went down to the camp to check on the *Molly,* not expecting to be able to get off yet (10 days on the skids). "Light winds" had been forecast, but was blowing up a 20 knotter from the West. Small craft warnings issued. Had let out slack last night for the "light winds" to carry her further down the skids a bit so maybe I could get ashore. What to my wonderment, I *could* shove her off, so I did and went to retrieve the motor and punt high on the skids. In the past days of wind and some sunshine I had opened the motor case and tried drying it out inside, cleaned the plugs and made sure the cord pulled. (Not "seized up" as is the ruinous case when seawater gets in). So I was hopeful it might start. Again to my wonderment I found I could *lift and carry* the motor, 8 steps at a time along the little dock. Got it *to and aboard* the *Molly* and she started!

Thrilled and proud of self, I left the Honda there and went to my long-abandoned mooring, fetched the lobster box and expected to find a dozen dead carcasses inside. They were all alive!! Only casualty in all this span of gales was one claw. I took the amputee and another with a tail wound ashore to be cooked first. Grabbed the laundry, beer bottles, empty kerosene, briefcase, etc. and raced ashore to get to the P.O. before Saturday closing time. Arriving at the C.V. wharf I realized I had left all the mail I'd written stacked on the cupboard shelf!

So, *two trips* to Shelburne from the island, in a rough westerly wind, but got the mail off finally at 3:45 P.M. and did the laundry. Then on to Susie and George with their surprise present. Stopped by at Tom's to ask about the *Molly*'s separating side braces, the punt's need for repairs – asked if he could build me another one, and he said he had one out back he'd sell me for $100. Thought I'd not get another wooden boat but I bought it on the spot. A beauty! The most graceful, dory-like punt I've ever seen, sturdy enough to carry the Johnson 15hp! So, while work is done on the *Molly* and punt and while I paint them I can be ferrying myself in the new boat. Where I'll keep all these boats I don't know. Will have to have a boat shed! The Honda can haul the new one up the slip at the light once Crofts leaves, or at Amos's – or at my new slip *when* it's built.

Came back in total darkness after the new moon had set and anchored off the camp dock. Will collect cargo with the cart in the morning. Read a letter from Aunt Ellen which said my hardships were so dire and *unnecessary* and *impossible*. She hoped I was dramatizing. Can't remember which "hardships" I wrote her about.

March 24

Beautiful morning! Frost rapidly vanishing. Will be sunny to +5(C) today. Need wood, must prune, but long to take time off for a sheep walk, and think I will. Haven't yet seen the sunk Coast Guard boat, or know how Crofts is faring. But watch me get sidetracked just bringing the wheelbarrow up the path from the fish house where I left it. Have also left little heaps of brush along the way.

Still haven't started my taxes. This is getting serious.

The first crocus! Little yellow ones in corners of the beds I dug and planted last fall. Removed the eelgrass mulch and spruce boughs and eelgrass from south walls and made a brush fence (temporary) to ward off the sheep. They're all back! Maude's here, looking pregnant, Grace still pregnant. Helen with her, Diana and Pauline. Kay still wanders about on her own with Chiquita, which is what Wanda and June must be doing elsewhere. A whole bunch of yearlings in lower orchard where I got sidetracked once again from pruning and taxes. Two with long tails and they weren't June.

Brought the *Molly* in to the camp dock and unloaded, left cargo there with wheelbarrow and Honda and cart waiting at the road. Gorgeous morning on the water. I sang love songs loudly in the cove, went on to the mooring and padded the loop where it was fraying. Then heard a Honda. Crofts and John arrived at the house with *my* Honda and cart full of stuff, Crofts "doing me a favour." I had been looking forward to walking back to the camp along the shore. He broke four bottles of beer along the way and dumped a gallon can of paint, denting it and filling the lid channels with dirt. I said nothing, thanked him and invited them in for coffee. Wondered later what Anne would have said in the same situation. John is leaving next week! Sigh. There goes dream of new landing and wharf. Then Crofts goes April 30. No extension now. Must be because of the sunken boat. He's been assigned next week to clear up the wood along the road and give me four-foot lengths. Must be the result of my letter.

Crofts said he'd had the worry of my being alone here on his mind all winter and had to check on me at least once a week. Baloney. Tried to sell me his horse, bridles, saddles, food pails and all for $300. A sweet horse, but encore baloney. No giveaway on his part. He's got to get the animal off the island. I said Van might take him if he'd give the horse away. I had to offer the use of my boat, as a gesture I guess, but I'm afraid Crofts will take me up on it.

New moon with the old moon in its arms … and, according to Sir Patrick Spens's crewman ["Sir Patrick Spens" is an eighteenth-century Scottish ballad] we should fear a goodly [deadly] storm. From the kitchen window, vivid starlight after the sun set touching the front apple branches, back where it was in October, I think.

March 25

Up in the apples trees again all day with minor digressions raking wood chips and bark. (Slugs are unwilling to crawl over bark, I read). "Northerly flow" is building to 20-30-knot winds tomorrow and Wednesday.

Crofts began his road clearing with a loud surge of chainsaw down the road on the dot of 8 A.M., but silence soon fell, a lengthy silence. Began to wonder if he'd come to grief and I should go looking after him. Then more chainsaw, sporadic through the afternoon but silent before and after 4 P.M., his heavy workday ended. I don't want to have to move the wood twice. A brush pile that will get bigger is where I want the wood put, out of the way of the shed. The view of stone walls, and the front field – to the side in back in separate piles for spruce, maple and birch logs. Then too, I can't get sidetracked with next winter's wood right now. Apple pruning has a deadline earlier than taxes, which is the only reason I'm not doing my taxes.

March 26

Mom and Dad's anniversary. 58 (?) years ago today they were on the train from B'ham [Birmingham, Alabama] with Bob Buswell (best man) headed for Charleston Gardens.

80F in the kitchen tonight on dead apple twigs! Again all day up in the apple trees, one old one high over the stone wall, but I was very careful and not at all uneasy.

LOVE being up in trees again. This whole experience is a magnificent regression.

... except for my aching, swelling right hand.

SO GRATEFUL TO J. S. BACH. Wish he would have a 300th Birthday more often.

Even Annabelle is reacting to the blissful music permeating the 80F house.

March 30

Coffee with Crofts and John has become a daily do except for yesterday (John's 50th birthday ... he looks 35) when I was ashore. This morning I slipped out to the pantry for milk and came back with his b'day surprise, a little round apple pie with red apple candle lit in the middle. He's leaving Monday and wanted a souvenir. As I've been apple pruning for three weeks I thought this appropriate (bought from the Lioness Bake Sale, or some such, at the Mall yesterday). (Margin Note: John blew out his candle without wishing, so I relit it for him. Then he made a silent wish, but said as he was leaving, when I said I wished he didn't have to leave (McNutt's) that he would come back – "That was my wish!" I told him my wish doubled the strength of his so maybe it would come true, but you're not supposed to tell your wishes. "Oh I don't believe in that," he said.)

Thursday was Mac's 11th birthday. He's still dangling his violet ribbons. I gave him a chocolate-chip muffin with lit candle, ringed by ham and cheese, outside on the little green bench next to the blooming crocus. All documented with Dad's "little camera."

Friday the usual hectic time in town, alleviated by a stroll with Tom Peterson down to his waterfront footage along a road he built himself descending steeply through birch and maple. He said for me to try out his boat before I paid for it. Sweet Tom. Incredibly honest and generous. Doesn't want me stuck with something that isn't right. I offered to lease it, wanted to give him something for it, but oh no. (Am sure I'll buy it, anyway. Too lovely to let go. I (underlined) could lease to Hal, et al. in the summers. I'm the opportunist that Tom is not.)

Reagan's MX missiles have won support of House and Senate, and AEP [likely American Electric Power] is advising its shareholders to vote against a proposition that they confront the acid rain issue square on with corrections, modifications, eliminations ... in their fuel waste practice ... and with reports on all actions to shareholders. I should sell my shares in AEP, and next, give up my citizenship.

Tony's letters and present of old liniment bottle he must have dredged with his oysters, packed in a Yarmouth salt cod box (and yards of yellow paper towel I can use) have me troubled. I grumbled about it while diddling with clearing up apple prunings, unable to sing in my usual fashion. Wanda (Lust) and June are back! – Helen, Grace, Sweetness, Maude, Diana, the yearlings and an untagged, long-tailed speckle-faced ewe yearling along with a tagged Suffolk-mix wether (missed in December.) – I love them all so, but they only tolerate me.

Am trying to fire Prizer Regal up to 400F to "bake fried chicken in Bisquick" – About to peal [peel] off layers.

Why troubled? I *know* all the reasons. Why have to enumerate here? Heard quoted on WQXR last night, "If you want the truth, never turn to a diary."/"journal"? Or did I read it in RD [*Rural Delivery*] book review of *Far Out Isn't Far Enough*?

Sins of omission.

I've found peace at last in solitude, joy in the fruits of this place, pleasure in fending for self, in hard physical labour (outdoors), fun with animals, apple trees and the people I chance to spend a few moments with, and I probably relish the mystery of my aloneness as it must appear to them. Nobody ever asks why, as I asked John this morning: "What's a good-looking man like you doing alone as a lightkeeper's assistant far from home for so long?" A loaded question. He blushed a little. I did not pursue. He said his children were the ones at the light. Poor sweet John. Speak of *mystery*. There's one. I wonder if he's an ex-con.

I need a hired man here but can't afford one. Can't afford to support Tony, either, in exchange for work, and it would be too demoralizing, for both of us.

If I can't be with the man I love, I'd *really* rather be alone. (Would enjoy having John here building a landing and wharf, though, for instance, hearing his melodious Cape Breton brogue and gently teaching him upper-class manners. That's different. Why? Read *Lady Chatterley's Lover* ... and I want to be free to carry on a love affair by correspondence with the Man in the Moon [Nick Lyons]. Tony's presence would change all that. A commitment, entanglement, I just don't want. But Joanna thinks I should give him a chance, and lord knows all friends and family would be delighted. That's half the trouble. Because I wouldn't be.

He says I'd have more time to write, but if he were here helping with the work, I'd be doing what I wouldn't have got to until next year and having to cook his meals at the end of the day, clean up after him and take his laundry ashore with mine (where I'd have to buy and lug twice as much food or shop twice as often). Nix. All for love, but nix for nutting –

April Fool's Day

March went out spectacularly yesterday, the sea dazzling and sparkling under the sun, sending great swells on a Southeast slant past the landing, while I climbed trees, moved wood and talked to the sheep ambling over the meadows as though there were actually something worth grazing on. The crocus were opening wide into multiple clusters of perky yellow and the tulips pushing through high with the daffodils. Robins under the apple tree in front, birdsong that took me back to Snedens and a nostalgic sense of well-being, all tied up with Mom and Dad but unidentifiable, in the cool bracing air combined with sunburn. I felt so well and alive. (Later Note: April Fool)

Today a SE gale is driving six inches of snow into airborne sheets, and one little tip of yellow, like the point of a crayon, pokes above the snow where it has drifted, sweeping it shallow at the corner of the flower bed.

The kitchen windows are all steamed up, so I can't be quite so easily distracted from starting my taxes *soon as* I clear the decks of business mail and obligations. Have the Franklin going. When the wind's from the east it heats the house with the bedroom closed.

April 2

Twenty years ago today I had a sprained ankle, insomnia, and the flu, and two tots hanging to either arm. I was moving into the house in Valley Cottage. Why must we be burdened with regrets for what is past, for fleeting youth?

The decks are cleared, both stoves warming the whole downstairs, winds light but not conducive to going ashore because six inches of snow covers the car and wharf on the other side. Shall I start my taxes? Or shall I go tackle that unsightly apple at the outside corner of the orchard wall? (Guess which? The apple tree, of course – and on the 3rd or 4th, I cleaned up cuttings and pruned two more trees by the lane.)

April 5 Good Friday and the full moon

I now know why I've procrastinated so long on my taxes. Not only the confusion of residence, NY State calling for 3 (underlined) forms, Revenue Canada, Farming Losses, Rental confusions (Evelyn Guye [real estate agent and appraiser in Shelburne] has utterly bollocksed the final statements, and official tax withholding statements, after 12 months of super-cautious, thorough accounting), 2 tenants in Valley Cottage, Capital Gains, 2 employers, office at home 2$^{1}/_{2}$ months, but the return of the pain of Howie's illness, that whole nightmarish period retold in a shoebox of receipts and letters, and the growing certainty that Francy has swindled me, collecting $2500 insurance coverage for *my* receipts he still does not return (Joyce [Francy's second wife] writes that they are still "corresponding" with London insurance company – since last May!) and under guise of benefactor, distributing *some* of the profit to Joanna and Howard. No more songs sung in the treetops. Am burning the whole Franklin woodpile of old punky spruce – but it's *dry* punk spruce, kept covered under plastic after long March-gales airing, while farms, schedules, instructions, statements, stubs and receipts litter the living room. Imagine this kind of morass here. So out of place.

Extreme low tide drew me to the shore to inspect the old landing at J's [Jonathan's] Point, to look for Howie's

Iranian pick I lost, and to gather mussels. This refreshed me, a mini vacation on McNutt's. Then back to the kick in the gut. A day for suffering. I haven't suffered enough lately. Too happy. Too lucky. Too lighthearted ... relieved so long from all this hideousness.

Jolly good I moved the split birch and February spruce into the shed when I did. This is the beginning of a *long* wet spell, methinks.

April 8

Rain, snow, hail, sleet, thunder et al. Bailed the *Molly* in the rain in the lee of an east wind. The landing is so bad, I wait for high tide to attempt to get the punt off and haul back up. Yesterday, Easter Sunday, the wind was too strong to go ashore and phone the kids, but I left the tax-table and climbed the apple by the lane. Got all the dead wood and some not dead, by mistake, and suckers, but can tell it's too late now to shock the trees with a proper pruning job. Filled some boxes of firewood, but not enough. It goes so fast. Finished burning the whole Franklin pile of old spruce on Saturday. Was seeing apple branches in my sleep and through the night. Also pulled a bunch of spruce seedlings and young trees, and got sidetracked – as usual – off the landing path. The whole business of pruning and clearing being a sidetrack from taxes, but I have to have wood.

Am back at the table now, and wondering if I can get enough heat on the top of the Franklin to steam cauliflower.

Little weather man has been giving ice-drift reports for northern waters since Thursday. They sound gruesome – A drifting polar cap, breaking open here and there, then closing again.

Still daylight at 7:30 P.M.! Doe, yearling, and faun at orchard brush pile, eating apple buds, I think.

Don't know what to write to Tony.

April 9

Finally managed to write Tony which said, among other pertinent assertions, all I have to say here: Can't work full-time at the taxes because I keep running out of dry wood and have to go a-pruning, and a-clearing and invariably getting sidetracked. Too late to prune much now, but dead wood and suckers. Buds are forming larger and the deer family was back again today at the brush piles.

Discovered a massive old tamarack that I didn't know we had. Needs care. Was evidently struck by lightning. How such a great tree has been here all along without my knowing it I can't say, but every day, with the clearing, I find more.

Two crows did a mating dance on the front yard outside the kitchen windows and pretended to object when they spotted Mac and me eyeing them.

Timmy brought me the hindquarters of a squirrel, first in several months, and I've just had it in garlic and wine.

From letter to Tony: "I am happier now, alone and working like an ant around the place, than I've been for many, many years. I sing love songs loudly from the treetops and out in the harbour and cove, but the thought of human entanglement stills the song in me ... How can you have a love song worth singing without entanglement? But I'm singing old tunes, from way back in the joyful past, songs I'd forgotten I knew, and others, unconsciously, that still honour a love lost. This great release has come after a long, dark winter, on the island, and in my life. I left a lot of hideousness behind, and nightmares, and am just now unfolding my wings. They may be made of gossamer, but they feel awfully good, and I've *got* to keep this light, free spirit now that I know what it can be."

April 10

Back in the trees again today when I should be doing taxes, but snow's coming tomorrow. I noticed tonight, as I collapsed in front of Prizer Regal while the mussels steam, that I have holes in everything … In my jeans, in my shirt, in my jacket (Howie's hooded sweatshirt which soon must go to the rag bag) and in my shoes.

I saluted the tamarack today after I cleared out in front of it, and its lower small dead limbs – There are mammoth lower dead limbs that reach way out into the forest and down to the ground in front, that have been struck by lightning, it seems – Split (clear) right* through underneath. I told the tree I was so sorry I hadn't seen it before the lightning struck, but then the afterthought: if I had known the tree, I would have been horribly upset.

*This use of the word "right" has been intriguing me. The Scotians use it all the time: "right close, right near, right clean, right safe," etc. – and we think that's odd, but we say "right now," "come right here," "They stay right together."

What more can you have but what you love?

A chapter on ECONOMY –

No need for money on the island because I can't spend a cent and don't want to. Never want to go ashore. Until I run out of something, or want something I don't have. (Once "want" meant "need," "be lacking of," but it doesn't anymore.)

April 21

Many days gone by in howling wind blast from the northeast. The mooring dragged. During the worst of this I retreated to the lee of J's bedroom and had the kerosene heater going all day while I caught up on mail from the mainland from the day before and wrote a long letter to Jogie and did up her birthday present. Last Sunday night I spent at Joan's, just managing to get ashore on a south wind and knowing it wouldn't freeze up for the first night since December. Left the cats out. The car wouldn't start in C.V. so had to get a new battery Monday morning. Dr. Jeffery Monday afternoon for the certification statement. He says I do have frostbitten toes, left foot, says my gnarled fingers are a form of "osteoarthritis" – Brought most of the mail back unopened, Nick's second letter among them, which turned out to be not the cozy missive I was looking forward to at bedtime but an urgent matter concerning Dad's copyrights and the plans of someone in South Carolina to reprint US & D and B.S. without permission. [*Upstream and Down* and *Big Stony*] Then came the gales. Nick's letter was written March 26 (I think). Couldn't get ashore until Friday April 19, to response [sic] with phone call to Nick and mail grams to the perpetrators. COLD WIND Tuesday – Thursday during which time Grace's lamb was born!

She vanished from the flock; and Mac and I went looking everywhere, I thought, between here and Indian Point to the North and the camp to the South. I somehow knew she was having it and would be close to home but never found her. Today I was struggling with the Honda, trying to start it by the side of the house where it has been fending sheep off from the tulips (Three chewed up already.) – when I glanced to the lower orchard and there was Grace out in the open high level place in the sun. I moved toward her, and sure enough a tiny, long-legged lamb with tiny black-speckled face came prancing behind her as she turned to move away. So much life and vitality, *happiness,* packed into a tiny newborn creature. It knew no fear, and frolicked and bounded while Grace sidled away muttering repeated maaahaah's in the direction of "Wether-or-Not," Maude's son, who rose resplendent for the occasion of Mac's and my approach, to protect his (obviously) own.

Later after sunset I went down again with both cats, and again Wether-or-Not held court at the top of the knoll, threatened Timmy and ushered Grace and lamb quickly down the knoll out of sight. Sweetness was with her, and other yearlings. Helen, who had kept close by her all of last week, was away at the North end with Wanda when I finally got there. Found a dead yearling of Ron's with a broken leg. Ghastly finish for that one. Probably fell down the same stone bank I'd seen the wethers fall down.

I opened up some tunnels for gathering, to clearings, with my pruning saw (which also cut the ear tag out of the dead yearling) and picked up a cartload of eelgrass for the 2nd half of the garden (still don't have enough) on the way back. People on the island. A yellow fishing boat at the wharf. *Perfectly beautiful day.* I tried again at the hollow ground along the shore with my elegant garden fork from Green Hand Tools, but could only dig down more than a foot through loose black soil and roots to a few small rocks.

Am moving in all directions around the place. Haven't finished the apple pruning, three to go in the far field, and all the lower orchard. Too late to do anything but take dead wood now. I pruned suckers from one lower orchard apple a week ago, was high up in the tree when Crofts and kids came down because somebody on the mainland was worrying about me. Joan. I hadn't been ashore, except for an evening of phoning Joanna at Skipper's, for three weeks.

Haven't finished my taxes. When I found I had an automatic extension, Evelyn Guye's tax figures were all mixed up, Francy hadn't returned the receipts and EBW sent Estate interest income records to arrive April 15, making the *whole* accounting so far wrong, I have just parked the whole thing. Took it ashore to Joan's and called Barry [her son, Elizabeth's chartered accountant] thinking I'd have to file a Revenue Canada and change the N.Y. State resident to non-resident, but he said, No, not till next year. Half the reason I retreated to the bedroom during the first and worst of the gales when I got back was that the taxes had made me sick.

Now I am back at the clearing of dead stuff from the path on into the field and between the path and the shore. Now is the time it must be done because all has died back to the ground and I can see what's dead and lying on the ground. I've found all kinds of things: an old skate (that clamps on a shoe), a stirrup, stove parts, wheels, etc. Want to prepare for a beach bonfire by getting the good firewood out of the dead stuff first and piling what's left, along with the *innumerable* spruce trees I've uprooted (seedlings and saplings, and larger that I've got with the pruning saw).

And meanwhile I have caulked thoroughly and am painting the *Blynken*. Want to get her in the water tomorrow to swell up and be ready to replace the other punt when it goes to Tom for repairs Tuesday, I hope. I'll leave the *Molly* at Sandy Point for him, too, and he'll deliver the new fourteen-footer to be my auxiliary boat if we can get together without telephone and without car.

It was so warm at the landing I stripped from shirt to undershirt to bra and finally topless, but oddly can't bring myself to take off long johns and socks yet. Probably the frostbite. Went all day today without lunch because I didn't want to open the fridge. It was cold inside from last night and will become so again tonight (I still have ice cubes from outside at night). No time to start the fridge because I'd have to pull it out from the wall and clean the fins and flue system. It's been off so long.

Dry holes for rhubarb I'm going to take from the Rennehan house tomorrow, divide and transplant. Have read that the early spring, when buds first appear, is the time for this. Ashes and manure in holes.

Daffodils are in full bud at the Rennehan house and at Louie's – Just beginning to bud here –

I'm so happy about Grace's little lamb. And so is she.

April 22

The day began so well: bright and still and warming rapidly. I dug up the rhubarb at the Rennehan place (saw many daffodil trying to push through from under the fallen wall to the west) and transplanted them, sliced by the spade, into holes I had fixed with manure and stove ash the night before. Moved eelgrass from the annex walls to the garden to finish bordering the new bed, pinning down the old orange tarp.

Then I found that the *Blynken* needed still more paint inside, so applied same, and Mac and I took off along the shore for a long-put-off sheep walk. Gathered some useful flotsam along the way, leaving it at Amos's where I also left Mac's leash by mistake. Moved on past the corral and began finding dead sheep at the Heannsler fields [later corrected to Atwood]. Not many. Enough to forewarn. Saw no new lambs, dead or alive, and the sheep (same bunch that hang out on the bar) not looking very pregnant. At the "Buoy on the tree" I decided to explore Grant 5 (Howie's) and the apple-tree clearing Waldo refers to as "Doane's." First found the cellar hole on a high knoll, and my little white-faced yearling, who was supposed to be "smart" according to Ron, dead in a comfortable place off under a tree. I don't think Waldo knows of the cellar hole. From there I found the apple trees and stone walls and decided that Howie has a gold mine here. Even the apples can be pruned back into shape.

Following sheep/deer trails, I came upon the "road" a short distance ahead, and turned back, clearing with the pruning saw and blazing tree trunks as I went. Then out again to the shore. Before long I found more dead sheep and the first dead lamb, pure white with black feet, back in the woods where I had never been before. Something seemed to draw me there. At Mousie's I found a dead ewe and dead twin lambs. At Hal's I found my "Sloop rock loner" dead, black and white. She was 3 years old and this would have been her first lamb.

Ahead were a large herd and one ewe was making the noise Grace made in the lower orchard, so I knew there were new lambs ahead. The other sheep all moved quickly on, but she stayed facing Mac and me and finally, after repeatedly looking down over the bank, moved on making noises all the while. My gaze, though, had been drawn to the border of trees where I saw what seemed an apparition, a seated lamb in plaster – the kind that sits out front in a tacky garden or in a cradle scene. [In pencil: It rose to meet Mac and wagged its tail.]

That little lamb, covered with its own dried afterbirth [In pencil: A dead twin nearby] is now in the tool shed. I tried to give it a bath. The poor thing already had pneumonia. But it was/is strong, struggled during the long walk home, and bleated here loud and clear, when it saw the other sheep. It has drunk half a bottle of evap[orated] milk and water and honey warmed with a little skimmed powdered added.

The ewe making the noise had tiny all-white twins whom she reluctantly left behind on the bank of stones with the ram. He stood perfectly still, watching Mac and me, while the *tiny* lambs held close to his side. Up ahead I saw another set of white twins frolicking after their retreating mother. The orphaned lamb had a dead twin nearby; there were two dead ewes down from him – one near the bank and one over it. I couldn't get their name tags and hold the lamb and mind the ram and twins all at the same time. I thought of standing the lamb alone in the field and waiting to see if a mother came along, but the only one making noises was mother of the twins with the ram, who stood still not far from us. The other ewes had all departed. I was afraid to upset the twins, ram and mother unduly, and afraid the little guy would die if I left him and moved on, so I turned about-face, held him close and carried him all the way home.

Mac hung directly at my heels the whole way. The lamb had stood up as we approached, on its shaky long legs, wagged its tail and moved straight for Mac, looking for something to nurse on. It had shied away from me. I almost had a problem catching it. Maybe if Mac hadn't been with me I wouldn't have been able to.

Never picked up the stuff I left at Amos's, nor explored the old house and grounds and road to the trail I cut to "Doane's" and thence to find my shepherd's crook I deposited somewhere in there.

The little guy is tucked in burlap bags, on top of the salt sack that washed up on the bar. He bleated loud and hard when I left him, but he had had all he would to drink – Am I going to stay awake through the night worrying about him and about God knows how many others that lie dead or barely surviving farther down the shore? I didn't even get up in #15. [Land grant #15. McNutt's is made up of mostly fifty-acre grants or lots.]

April ~~24~~ 25 (Don't even know the date)

It's all getting beyond me. Little Guy needs his ba-ba every four hours, 6-8 ounces, and I wonder how in heaven I'll ever get things done ashore. Winds are picking up again. Tom has the punt which I delivered to Sandy Point Tuesday, when I thought the *Blynken* would be ready, but the water gushed out of it, bottom center where the bottom strakes got in the way of the caulk. Will have to look again from the inside – Didn't leave the *Molly* because the wind had become strong for a maiden voyage in the blue boat, which I towed back with me anyway, and damn good thing I did. I can haul it up the landing (just) and it's high, light and dry but not good for pulling alongside a pounding boat at mooring. Its thole pins nearly got snapped off. I think I've already cracked and split a few pieces here and there. The *Molly* has leaked profusely ever since beating into the wind going to Sandy Point.

As if boats weren't enough problem, the Honda now doesn't run. Waldo and Guys came to paint the camp and I made the mistake of turning the handbook and "oil seal" over to him to install. He read the wrong page, thought it was too big but might fit back behind somewhere, and on my prompting turned the timing screw; the only way to get the thing off, it seemed. But the whole pulser turned with it. Anyway, he apparently didn't set it back right. I drove the Honda and cart back down to the camp this A.M. with the book, to show him the page that illustrates how to get down to the oil seal (and beyond) but they had left, and the Honda stalled the moment I stopped. Which did not seem right.

I checked the oil according to the book's instructions for the first time, and found it is low on oil so decided this seal had better get in there. But when I took the cap off, the pulser was shifted sideways. The thing wouldn't start at all, and acted funny. I saw the way the pulser seems to go in the book and turned it to that position and she almost started. Then nothing at all. Maybe by now she's only flooded, but I'm afraid we've wrecked the works again, and I'm annoyed with Will Butler. He should have made sure the oil seal was intact in the first place. Now I have to see him in town, as well as Tom, who never picked up the caulk I had for him because after I'd waited an hour and a half for him, I went into John Goodick's to chat, or phone Susie again if need be, and even though we were looking out the window we missed seeing him arrive. Saw him take off up the road with my punt in the back of his truck.

And the clearing job grows and grows the more I do. I'm seeing dead bay branches when I close my eyes. I keep filling cartons for the stove, emptying them each day and filling them again, with dead bay and alders, the brush piles billow out higher and wider, and the areas to be cleared seem to extend on beyond forever.

The apple trees have been abandoned in the far field and lower orchard. I did manage to clean up the back of the middle field, pull all the spruce seedlings, lop the rest, and saw and rake where I'd left a mess at the last big apple. The bog still sports its spruce to be lopped, fingers pointing up here, there, and everywhere in our view of the water, and the high dead bay still mottles the budding crowns with white and gray in the far field. These and the spruce in front were to be the clearing job initially, and ten months later they still have not been done.

I owe several important letters, several personal, still have not mended the chimney wall and cupboard, cleaned and repaired the sewing machine, the yard chairs, have abandoned my taxes, and have not begun the garden cultivating, planting and fence building, the moving of wood and the painting of boats! (Then there's spring cleaning, and window painting … small oversight.) However … as I cleared some patches along the path through the meadow, and Mac looked after Little Guy for me, very well indeed, to earn his puppy biscuits, and Little Guy would wake up and gallop toward me, shaking his ears and bellowing "Maaa!" and as Timmy and Annabelle leapt about the stone walls and Chiquita, Jennifer, and one orphan wether grazed quietly nearby, and as the wind diminished and the sea dazzled, I felt so blessed and happy. It didn't matter that my forearms were scratched raw and that horns pierced my socks far down in my shoes.

Tonight I washed my hair in the basins and took a bath in the sink with room to spare. Have gotten quite skinny in the hips.

April 27

Well, I wrote it all to Howie, of giving up "Little Guy" in the moonlight to a flock of wild sheep that presumably contained his real mother come to reclaim him … His tiny figure alone on the crest of the knoll by the cellar hole, alone among ghosts and quietly facing a host of advancing, purposeful wild sheep. But I didn't tell how I stood there, too, with Little Guy at my feet before I retreated to let him and his mother be reunited, and how I cried out to the four-legged woolly dam: "Why didn't you take better care of him? The poor thing was abandoned, covered with dried-up slime! I thought you'd rejected him. Or died. Here, take him. Hurry up. Don't dilly-dally. Take him and be good to him!" Nor how I heard the snuffling shuffling advance in the moon shadows of a pack of sheep that didn't like me at all. Finally they frightened Little Guy – as much as they did me, and he turned and galloped to me yelling, "Maaa!" Later, the one with the heart-wrenching bleat followed us to the house, and once again in the moonlight I repeated my tender farewells to Little Guy. I got down on all fours and edged him toward the waiting sheep.

(Continued next week, same time, same station) When Little Guy at last advanced to nuzzle the fleece of the big sheep in the dark, he wasn't impressed with what he found and trotted back to me. The sheep then turned reluctantly away, revealing its long tail – a yearling wether that had missed December's gather!

Mac is working hard to earn his puppy biscuits looking after Little Guy, and L.G. trots alongside the wheelbarrow just as the other new lambs travel alongside their mothers.

Put the motor on Tom's blue boat and we skittered over the water, barely touching it. A hover craft rapid transit to Carleton Village. Am frigging with the Honda, a worrisome business of misaligned pulser and timing. Put caulk gun and more paint to the bottom of the *Blynken* and hope to heaven she's tight. Both the *Molly* and the blue boat are now on the hunters' skids – filling their landing.

April 30

What a noisy place this is at sunset! The gulls have been making tentative summer sounds for several days, but tonight they set up a fracas of all sorts of wild and loony noises, while a real loon joined in (one I saw yesterday just off the boat landing), whippoorwills were heard before all this moved into crescendo, seals barked, and finally the first willets took over with loud and extensive pilly-wee-wees, a homecoming to mark Joanna's birthday.

Her day was memorable here on several other counts: I removed my long johns for the first time (other than the day in Shelburne when I visited Dr. Jeffery – I put them on again to sail back home). Felt so odd at first, as though I had shed an outer skin and was fleshy and vulnerable. I got used to it fast enough, working in the heat removing all the eelgrass and spruce bough wreathings from the house. A lot of the eelgrass went to mulch the gooseberries and currants after I buried them in horse manure. Then with the boughs I made brush fences, new wreaths, encircling the bushes and so far it's kept the sheep away.

Lord, what a lot of sheep: Two flocks, with three rams, from down yonder, and our own, with Grace and lamb returning. I looked up from the brush pile to see Mac in a nose-to-nose confrontation with the lamb, and soon to be a horn-to-nose, with Grace advancing. Oddly, the other sheep hung back in a watchful, silent semi-circle. They knew Mac well, and know our Little Guy by now (asleep on his burlap sleeping-bag-beddies in the shed) but were most curious.

Also of note today, I pulled out a yard chair and stool for the first time (only two don't need repairs) and sat in it, stripped topside and had a beer. Even my inhibited frost-bitten toes bared themselves for the occasion. And most important today, Crofts and I saved the life of Diana's yearling, the little Suffolk mix that holds her tail up as she prances off, just like her mommy. Crofts had found her dying of bloat (trapped on her side) at the north end. We harnessed her upright to an apple tree and I fed her milk and honey through the night, exercising her legs. This morning she walked off and grazed all day. (Margin Note: The day is also unhappily memorable as the first birthday of Joanna's when I have not even spoken to her. The wind didn't let up enough for Tom's small boat until 8 P.M. and I knew she would have gone out by then so I didn't cross over to phone her.)

McNutt Island Journal 5
May 1, 1985 – [May 22; entries for January 1, 1987; undated; September 28, 1988]

May 1

The yellow daffodils I planted last November are out full, all fresh and perky behind a barricade of spruce boughs, wrung ladder, green table, barbed wire roll, old hoe, old green wheelbarrow and whatever else can fend off a sheep between now and fences. Fifty sheep must come and go past here daily now. I don't understand it. Could it be the lure of the lamb?

The radio batteries have been dead for three days. I haven't the foggiest notion what's happening in the world, although I guess it's only more of the same with [Ronald] Reagan and his wreaths for Nazi grave sides and aid to Nicaragua, and have discovered that I don't want to know. I could scrape up four batteries that would receive well enough at night, if I combed the house, but it just isn't worth the trouble.

Tried to preserve and protect the currants and gooseberries in the lower orchard and by the back wall today. A simple task that was to take only the morning, but I worked until 8 P.M. on it because in the process of gathering eelgrass, sheep drops, lopping trees for brush fence … I of course browsed off to clear the corner by the well, a nasty mean patch of roses that either didn't want me there or didn't want to let me go, pulled up all the spruce and tamarack seedlings, and did a sizable job on the spruce in the bog in front. Looked for fiddleheads. The big ones aren't up yet, though the thin ferns are all uncurling. Little Guy romped and slept by me all day while Mac was intermittently serious lamb-sitter, bored or jealous. Timmy has been gone for three nights; consequently Annabelle purrs constantly, unless she's hissing at the lamb.

May 7

Maybe I've let so many days elapse because I didn't want to count how many Timmy had been gone. Mac and I went to the camp three times looking for him. I retraced the old open well in the woods, combed the shore and camp landing for remains of a marine accident, but this morning he was on the cellar door at the kitchen window. Wet but lean and fit, without so much as a scratch. I wonder if he'd been staying with the Crofts all along.

They are now gone, and I am sole inhabitant of McNutt Island. It feels rather good. Spent yesterday with a beach bonfire while the helicopter crossed over and back, dangling huge nets full of goods directly overhead, about two dozen times. Maybe Crofts thought the bonfire was my farewell to him; fact is, conditions were ideal for the first time: east wind, wet ground, low tide late afternoon so I had from 2 to 9 P.M. to burn, and I cleared the whole shore, branches for more view of the landing and several spruce trees to boot which went up with a roar of cascading sparks as a sort of finale. Then hisssssss, dense smoke cloud, and done with. A safe fire, cleaned up afterward by the east wind and outgoing tide.

Also planted bachelor's buttons and snapdragons in the flower beds, the latter being so minuscule I couldn't see them spill from the package. Lord knows where they are.

Little Guy had his first, and repeated, scolding for hopping in the garden but I think he was frightened by the helicopter.

It's good to have Timmy back. I really missed him. And he's my living tie to Dad.

May 21

Ollie [a herring gull Joanna raised when she was thirteen] has come home to die; eleven years after being raised in a box by the kitchen stove he now lies there dead, a smile on his beak, light in his eye, poised as if in full swim, at rest at last after two days of heavy-laboured breathing.

Howie is home after O-D'ing on junk food and beer, and not taking his vitamins for two weeks, a relapse into schizophrenia and back to square one, salvaged by a distraught sister and Joe Hyde [Francy's brother and a famous chef in Snedens Landing] who brought him here. Before the news reached me via the new lightkeepers (Crofts never told me he was being replaced for three months) I was at extreme loose ends, unable to follow a job through to completion, distracted, not sleeping, unable even to write in this journal. When the message came to call Joanna, "It's important," I knew Howie had crashed.

But he's here and fast on the mend, building me a garden fence – clearing the upper pasture for the posts and poles along with Jerry and Vandee O'Neil (lightkeepers) for $5 per hour. He takes his vitamin regimen and Trilafon three times a day, stays off milk, sugar, wheat, caffeine and alcohol (snitched the brandy first night and plunged.) – I've cut out the Cogentin and he sleeps better, is less restless, and seems perfectly normal most of the time. Didn't hear a single paranoid thought uttered today.

The sad little wether died. Van never came for him. I would have set him free once his droppings were better, but thought Van was coming to collect him. Didn't give him enough water, and he would tangle in the chain, which must have weakened him. He's at rest in the forest, looking very sweet and *healthy*. I feel so bad about him.

Ollie will join him tomorrow, where the crows don't seem to go.

Little Guy now takes 12 ounces of milk three times a day and still expects his "late night ba-ba." He gallops after me everywhere and grazes while I work outside. He had a bad bout of diarrhea. I kept him in his shed several days. Now he grazes hard, like a grown-up sheep, on rose and raspberry. Whatever made him sick he seems to be avoiding.

Jerry manoeuvred the fallen brick flue (unused brick from the Rennehan place with the help of the jeep, Vandee and me, the Honda and cart, and Joe began building the guest room flue. He and Joanna were here only three days. They say they'll return June first.

It was odd, and still is, cooking for someone else. I'm sociable enough, and still an attentive, loving mother, but I've ceased to function well as hostess/provider.

May 22

New moon tonight, all the gulls at Jonathan's Point gathered for Ollie's wake. They must be the family he has left behind.

New buds unfurled on the oak, maple and birch, pale green leaf on the apples, fiddleheads high, terns making an uproar on the bar. (Red and yellow tulips have been making a splendid show.)

Out of milk and dog food. Underwear for Howard. Must go ashore. Gale following Friday. Want to look for morels [a type of edible mushroom] and finish clearing the far field. Do not wish to go ashore for harried, rushed errands in between "ba-ba's," but haven't been ashore (excluding last Monday at 5 P.M. for groceries before H, J. & J arrived) for over two weeks.

So much drama in the animal world it fills my time. Chiquita, my grandest yearling, is dangling her fleece from below her neck and looks like a plucked black chicken. "Sweetness" has worms. What will become of us all? Ollie knows. So does the wether.

New Year's Day – 1987 –

Maybe one day I'll be able to fill the lapse. People have interposed. Horror, sorrow, struggle, hope and joy. My animals go on, but some do not, lost to what we bring into their world or lost to our misguided efforts to cure for and heal. Gretchen. Heidi. Nellie. *Annabelle.* Little Lamb. And now Tilly. The story of a young sheep.

Cliff's boat was off the shore, hauling traps, coming to our bloodied snow at just the wrong time. He must have heard the keening of an Indian and seen me trying to stop my mouth with my hand.

Chaquita is Tilly's big sister. She is Margarita's mother and Che's lamb from three years back. Che's lamb this year was a ram, turned wether at the shearing gather, and sent by me, just before Christmas, to the firing squad. I was never made to be a farmer, but I am.

(undated)

Scattered notes and one year's engagement calendar do a poor job of filling in the gap ... Garden journal begun in spring of 1988.

September 28, 1988

A small flounder dropped on the woodpile tarpaulin in the cool, damp hours before the sun lifts. Back in over the trees somewhere an osprey was pretty miffed about it, but we had a delicious pan fry for breakfast, with parsley and lemon. Timmy got the head. I also sacrificed some of the skin and a hunk of meat along the fin bones for him because he came in while I was cooking with the fifth squirrel in five days, this one bigger than the other four. Squirrel stew two nights in a row. Every ingredient but the salt, pepper, flour and olive oil from McNutt's: Potatoes, carrots, onions, *ripe tomatoes,* celery, garlic, parsley, thyme, bay leaf, peas and/or parsnip and turnip. (Peas the second night with leftovers.) I'm glad I went early to uncover the woodpile. A welcome change in the menu.

Our oak tree, the only one on the island, is putting out acorns now. If I don't take Timmy soon to Jordan Bay I foresee too many nights of squirrel stew. They must be lured to the acorns from all over the island, because surely we didn't have this many squirrels left after Timmy's summertime rambles. I hear them chattering in the trees all around the house, setting up a chorus, maybe, in memorial service for lost lovers and friends.

About the Author

Elizabeth Walden Hyde was a teacher, an actress, a writer, an avid journal-keeper, and a sheep farmer. Born in Palisades, New York, she enjoyed a joyful upbringing in Snedens Landing and married her childhood friend, Francois (Francy) Tonetti Hyde. She spent a year in Africa during her marriage. Her unpublished novel, *Not Even The Moon*, concerned this period in her life.

Elizabeth purchased land on McNutt's Island with a hundred-dollar wedding gift and spent summers there with her family. She and Francy later divorced. In 1984, she decided to winter on the island, without electricity or indoor plumbing. Over two winters, she tackled the myriad tasks required to keep herself, her dog, and two cats warm and comfortable in her "little red house," including regular trips to Shelburne for supplies, even in bitter winter weather. In between herculean jobs like chipping ice from her boat, chopping and splitting wood, digging wells, and insulating the upstairs of the house, Elizabeth revelled in visits from her children, Joanna and Howard, the freedom of climbing trees, being outside with the wildlife, the companionship of her cats Timmy and Annabelle, looking after her sheep, and the good humour of her faithful Mac, a white-haired terrier mix.

Though the diagnosis of a terminal brain tumour cut short her active and varied life, Elizabeth is remembered as someone who lived with vigour and enjoyment. Her ashes were scattered in the Lower Orchard at her McNutt's Island home by her son Howard, where a plaque and a stone squirrel offer a reminder of this vibrant, adventurous, and courageous woman.

About the Editor

Joanna Gilman Hyde is an artist and writer living on Nova Scotia's South Shore. Born in New York, she spent her youth in Rockland County, heading to Nova Scotia during the summers with her family. She holds a Bachelor of Fine Arts from The Cooper Union for the Advancement of Science and Art (1983). In 1984, she painted *Self-Organizing Galaxy*, a 10,000-foot temporary canvas art installation, on the roof of 5 World Trade Center, where the colourful spiral design contrasted with the surrounding concrete urban environment. A prolific painter, she exhibits her artwork at various locations in the Shelburne area.

Joanna's talents are not confined to canvas alone: she and her first husband, Peter Haeghaert, restored The Shakespeare House in Shelburne for her mother, Elizabeth. Joanna, herself the mother of two children, feels a deep connection to coastal Nova Scotia, where she always envisioned a life as a successful artist. It has been her home for thirty-five years, and she regularly enjoys the sight of wildlife in her front yard. Visit her poetry blog at joannagilmanhyde.com.